LETTERS TO HOME:

ART AND WRITING BY LGBTQ+ NIKKEI AND ALLIES

This book contains mature themes that may not be suitable for some audiences, please use discretion when reading.

Printed in the United States of America
First Printing, 2024
ISBN 979-8-218-43180-8

The articles, written pieces, creative works, and additional editorial content in *Letters to Home: Art and Writing by LGBTQ+ Nikkei and Allies* do not necessarily reflect the views of the editors, the larger Okaeri organization, other Okaeri-affiliated members, or Okaeri's fiscal sponsor LTSC.

"Okaeri has been an important resource and support for many LGBTQ+ Japanese Americans, including me. This book is a great reflection of this community and its ever growing pride. *Letters to Home* will provide a unique sense of belonging wherever you are. Please read it and feel the warmth and welcome of coming home."

- George Takei
AUTHOR, ACTOR, ACTIVIST

"Provocative, ground-breaking and all-inclusive, even in its offerings in the Japanese language—*Letters to Home* breaks any preconceived notions the public and Japanese Americans have about the current status of the Nikkei LGBTQ+ community. Congratulations go to the editors for crafting a gorgeous and well-considered publication that honors the spirit of Okaeri."

- Naomi Hirahara
NATIONAL BEST-SELLING AUTHOR OF THE MARY HIGGINS CLARK
AWARD-WINNING *CLARK AND DIVISION*, AND THE MAS ARAI MYSTERY SERIES

"Okaeri's literary gathering *Letters to Home* continues its tradition of bringing us in and lifting up the Nikkei LGBTQ+ diaspora, through an expansive and gorgeous collection of poetry, art, essay and photography. Every piece is a proclamation, each voice a profound expression—showing the wild diversity of our experiences while allowing us to find in each other, and this anthology, a collective mirror and a chosen home."

- traci kato-kiriyama
AUTHOR OF *NAVIGATING WITH(OUT) INSTRUMENTS*;
DIRECTOR/CO-FOUNDER OF TUESDAY NIGHT PROJECT

"It's such an honor to journey together with Okaeri on this path for peace, compassion, love, kindness, and dignity for our children and all living things! Your book, *Letters to Home*, captures so much of what I hope for our world. Please keep up your great work...."

- June Kuramoto
MUSICIAN AND SONGWRITER, HIROSHIMA
2024 NATIONAL ENDOWMENT FOR THE ARTS RECIPIENT

EDITORIAL TEAM & ACKNOWLEDGEMENTS

Managing Editors
Michael Matsuno
Cody Uyeda
Rino Kodama

Graphics & Layout Designer
Daniel Tomita

Submissions Manager
Kevin Mori

Supporting Editorial Team
Marsha Aizumi
Wayne Itoga
Kai Mita
Deena Umeda

Cover Art
"Okaeri: Mail to Michiyo Fukaya" by Mitsuko Brooks

Okaeri would also like to acknowledge and thank Mia Barnett, Mizuki Shiraishi, Keith Nishida, Bryan Takenaka, Eric Arimoto, Aya Yabe, Bill Watanabe, and the rest of the Okaeri community for their input, feedback, and support throughout this process.

TABLE OF CONTENTS

Change Is Everywhere 11

Sam Nakahira

Introduction: The Shared Space of Writing & Artmaking 12

Michael Matsuno

The Beginning: A History of Okaeri 20

Marsha Aizumi

01 – WELCOMING

A Long Welcome 38

Feet 42

Chrysanthemum Play 45

3,000 year bath 48

Things I think of when I think of my father 52

02 – THE EARTH AND THE BODY

Surippa/スリッパ 62

藍色 63

because our roots find each other underground 64

Freesia 67

tadaima 70

coffin, 2042 73

Finding Authenticity as a Queer, Nikkei Dancer 76

Every Body Has a Story 80

03 - REFLECTIONS OF PRIDE

What is Pride? 86

Shared Experience is a Helluva Drug 89

A Vagabond's Life (Without the Romance):
A Polemic on the Meaning of Home 95

tempus fugit 107

Living Your True Self 111

オカエリ短歌集 115

Going Home 118

帰路につく 128

04 - SELF-PORTRAITS

On Fairies and Dust 138

Becoming Sakura 142

(Un)broken 147

我慢して(≠ 頑張って!) There are two kinds of
perseverance 150

Untitled (self-portrait) 153

A Prodigal Son's Return to the Village: A Reflection
on Growing up Gay in (and Out) of the Nikkei
Community 157

Finding My Way Home 168

05 - WHERE WE FIND HOME

My Aloha 174

Finding Pride in Fargo 177

Softening Steel 182

The Shape of Okaeri 189

「お帰り」の形 192

This is Me 194

Finding Community, Building Community 198

Charting Shame and Silence: Transforming into
    Radical Softness and Self-Celebration 203

When I get home 210

06 – THE IMPERFECT PRACTICE OF PARENTING AND ALLYSHIP

To My Dearest One 216

おかえり 218

おかえりイラスト解説 222

幸せへの一番の近道 A Shortcut to Happiness 225

The Golden Rule & the Spirit of Okaeri: A Lesson
    from my Mother 228

Listen 236

The Evolutionary Journey of Mothering 241

Our Story in Translation 246

Crossed up in Translation 256

Meetings At The Shore 263

Glossary 266

Author & Editorial Team Biographies 272

Resources & Supporting Okaeri 291

INTRODUCTION:
THE SHARED SPACE OF WRITING & ARTMAKING
Michael Matsuno

Ananda, you have invited me to walk in meditation with you, but when we do walk, we chatter and laugh endlessly about everything, foolish nonsense, and yet with the pleasure of the deepest sense of our living moments together; we live a noisy meditation. I suppose we would not have it any other way. To be honest, the silent meditation we experience is when we are apart, distant in our own worlds, writers in separate universes. That is perhaps the state of the writer and the letter writer, a meditative state graced by the imagination of the presence of the other.

Karen Tei Yamashita
Letters to Memory, 112

This excerpt from Karen Tei Yamashita's *Letters to Memory*, an epistolary memoir on the legacies of Japanese American incarceration, recasts the act of writing as a form of meditative communion with imagined others. Yamashita does this very thing by invoking ancient muses to help her make sense of the archive of letters and artifacts she inherited from her extended family. Here, the author addresses Ananda, the Buddha's disciple revered for his powers of memory and preservation, in examining her family's art collection. Among the acquired works are her grandmother's paintings, made in the long days of isolation in the Topaz relocation center. She wonders aloud if artmaking provided escape for her grandmother and the artists at camp, a means of accessing the "meditative solace of nature." Thus, Yamashita views both painting and writing as inherently solitary endeavors that paradoxically provide an inner sense of togetherness.

So too does this volume take a variety of expressive forms—essay, autobiography, poem, portrait, and performance—as silent meditations with absent loved ones. In this light, such practices are both confined and collaborative. Though they may be created in isolation, they often engage the very people to whom we most desperately wish to speak. In writing about our identities and experiences, like Yamashita, we may be listening most keenly to the voices of our past. Or perhaps, like the individuals in this volume, we unknowingly address many Anandas all at once: mothers, fathers, daughters, brothers, faith leaders, lovers, friends, places, future selves. We, the editors, sought to create a platform for Queer *Nikkei* and allies to share such private correspondences with a broader community. In turn, we ask how might these works form a larger, collective meditation? What imaginary presence graces us all? How can we find togetherness through literary acts that define our solitude?

Letters to Home

This volume addresses a particular community and its need for self-expression by bringing together writing and art by LGBTQ+ *Nikkei* and allies. It is a project organized by Okaeri, an advocacy group for Queer Japanese and allies living in the US and abroad, and collectively produced by a committee of volunteers. Our call for submissions asked contributors to reflect on their interpretations of the Japanese phrase, "*okaeri*" ("Welcome home" or "Welcome back"), as it relates to their lived experiences as Queer *Nikkei* and allies. We encouraged individuals to explore topics, both positive and negative, relevant to identity and community acceptance. Works in this large collection represent a wide range of voices, from experienced artists to nonprofessional writers. Many of these contributors reside in various parts of California, close to where the organization is based. However, the project reached Japanese people of all ages living in Hawai'i, Minnesota, New York, Pennsylvania, Texas, and various parts of Japan.

In creating our call, we decided it was important to provide a platform for both Queer and ally individuals, thereby reflecting the core values of the organization. The everyday expression, "*Okaeri!*" invokes a household, a shared place of living. Indeed, this utterance is essential to our mission of creating a better, safer world for Lesbian, Gay, Bisexual, Trans, Queer and Non-binary Japanese people of all ages. As Okaeri's founder Marsha Aizumi writes, the name reflects the hope that "no matter how long or how far you had traveled from the JA community, you are able to return and be welcomed." For this reason, family and allyship take a critical role in the construction of a livable, compassionate place for Queer gathering. Okaeri aspires to promote the understanding that such an environment can only be created when everyone under the same roof participates in this gesture. These aims reinforced our desire to curate a volume that reflected all *Nikkei* voices: LGBTQ+, parent, and ally.

Letters to Home responds to the important role storytelling and personal reflection appears to play in Japanese diasporic communities. We leave empirical understandings of this cultural phenomenon to scholars of a different kind. However, Yamashita offers our project a useful poetics of writing, one that views composition as both a solitary operation and a means of communicating with our imaginations. Writing and artmaking allow us to experience togetherness even without its physical presence. This volume therefore proposes a different mode of gathering and an alternative view of Okaeri as an organization. More than just its 42 authors, these pages are graced by the countless individuals who inhabit their private imaginations. Viewing such a space as infinitely accommodating, writing provides room for celebration and bereavement, not in isolation, but in the inviting presence of others.

Insofar as these inner dialogues are specific to each author, the ideas they produce are diverse. No two individuals agree entirely on a stable definition of home, nor the feelings it evokes. In her poem on returning to Oʻahu, for example, Jill Togawa describes a scene with her parents in which a fragrant breeze ("Feel the *anuhea*") drifts through an open window. Togawa thus locates her sense home in the sensorial pleasures of its inviting climate. No such romanticism exists in Wayne Itoga's essay, although details of his lifelong independence are infused with unexpected poetry. Home is many things. "Something outside of me like bell bottoms or hoop skirts." Itoga examines a broad series of minutiae, mundane artifacts of life that carry and enforce socially accepted connotations of what home ought to be. Meanwhile, Tomo Hirai explains how she experiences *okaeri* in the process of connecting over shared interests. "Are you plural? Autistic? A furry? Do you play the critically acclaimed MMORPG Final Fantasy XIV ... ?"

Works in this volume highlight how acceptance can sometimes be incomplete. Tsukuru Fors writes, "I always felt that Japan was my birth mother who never loved me back, whereas the United States of America was my adopted mother who embraced me, albeit with lots of issues of her own." Likewise, parents and allies reflected on past mistakes and new understandings. Queer children grappled with self-image. In this view, *okaeri* is never quite a perfect gesture, and accepting it can be equally complicated. Underlying many of the works in this volume is a sense of personal accountability for these negotiations, whether it be extending invitations or receiving them.

It is worth mentioning that these ideas permeated our work as a committee. Indeed, collaborating on a project of this size routinely required willingness to compromise and openness to welcome in new ideas. Included among our collective occupational labels are ceramicist, writer, musician, graphic designer, organizer, and activist. This produced a dialogue informed by many perspectives and opinions, as well as occasional disagreements. The trials and rewards we faced demonstrated for us how our lived enactments of *okaeri* are entangled in the messiness and misunderstandings of human interaction. We allowed our own evolving notions of community to guide how we engaged with the material entrusted to us, and hope that it is reflected in the overall gesture of togetherness made by this volume.

Themes

Works in this volume have been organized into six major sections outlined below. In general, the contributions we received tended to fall into four categories: art, poetry, essay, and short story. Grouping pieces by genre, however, offered limited commentary on their ideas and failed to highlight the wide range of perspectives that informed them. Instead, we based our organization loosely around a handful of emergent themes directly inspired by the texts. Sections therefore include a mix of literary and art-based approaches. They each combine voices from across generations and represent an assortment of LGBTQ+, family, and ally perspectives in dialogue with one another. Given that topics and motifs trace intricate constellations across this large body of work, our grouping is just one of many potential arrangements. Our aim with this ordering was to nurture thoughtful reflection, and to inspire new connections by the reader.

01 - WELCOMING

Works in this opening section evoke ceremonial rituals from the ancient past to the present, from widespread social customs to intimate practices. Each piece offers a perspective on the power of ritual to create and sustain a sense of belonging, sexuality, and interpersonal connection.

02 - THE EARTH AND THE BODY

This section focuses on topics related to the natural world. Several authors deal with the earth's elements and its fertility as a source of identity, while others explore the intricately woven patterns of physical embodiment.

03 - REFLECTIONS OF PRIDE

Here, pride is understood broadly to encompass a kaleidoscope of thoughts and emotions related to LGBTQ+ identity. Authors explore their inwardly directed attitudes and reflect on the people, places, and events that have shaped their positive self-perceptions.

04 - SELF-PORTRAITS

The poetry, art, and storytelling in this section are all seen as self-portraits of some kind. These autobiographical illustrations often involve elements of fantasy, imagination, and multiplicity.

05 - WHERE WE FIND HOME

This section responds to a major theme of movement across geographical space. Authors in various life stages reflect on transformations associated with departures, arrivals, and returns. In total, these works cast family and queer community as inextricably tied to perceptions of place.

06 - THE IMPERFECT PRACTICE OF PARENTING AND ALLYSHIP

This final collection of writing offers a variety of perspectives on allyship and parenting. Authors embrace growth and human nature as necessary features of these roles. Collectively, these works demonstrate ways in which parents and allies hold themselves accountable for creating safe and healthy environments for loved ones.

THE BEGINNING:
A HISTORY OF OKAERI
Marsha Aizumi

My dream for Okaeri started with just one thought back in 2013. Why is there no visibility in the Japanese American (JA) community for LGBTQ+ people and families? What a difference that would have made to Aiden—my transgender son, me, and our family. What a difference that could make for other JA families. But where do we start? I didn't know what the first steps were, I didn't know what it would become, and I didn't know who to talk to. All I knew was a seed was planted. A small spark was lit and the warmth of the idea overcame me. It made me feel excited.

I always believe that if I follow my heart, it will lead me in the right direction. I might meet someone who could help me, or introduce me to a person, or just be a cheerleader of my dream. This has happened over and over again, and so I had faith that when the time was right, I would be led to the right people.

One of the names that kept coming up for me was Bill Watanabe, former executive director and co-founder of the Little Tokyo Service Center (LTSC), an LA-based non-profit organization that provides a comprehensive array of social welfare and community development services. One person called Bill, "Mr. Little Tokyo," not only because LTSC was in Los Angeles' Little Tokyo area, but also because of his passion and connection to the Little Tokyo community and organizations. When people spoke his name, there was a deep respect and appreciation for this man. But I did not know him.

As fate would have it, I saw a post on Facebook about a group called Asian American Pacific Islander Christians for Social Justice (AAPI CSJ). They were doing an event about LGBTQ+ individuals and Christians. Since Aiden and I were rejected by a Christian church in the city we lived in, I was intrigued by an Asian group advocating for LGBTQ+ issues and bringing in a gay Japanese minister to speak. At the last minute I decided to attend. As I walked into the meeting room filled with Asian faces, I felt optimistic. Then, the event started. Walking up to the podium was a distinguished, gray haired man with a warm and relaxed manner. When he introduced himself, I took in a deep breath of amazement. His name was Bill Watanabe.

Bill started his introduction by saying this was not a space to debate LGBTQ+ issues, but to hear the story of a gay minister. In his calm and objective way, Bill laid the foundation for the event to be a safe space. As I listened to the story of Rev. Melvin Fujikawa, I was moved by so many things he said. But the thought that stayed with me was how he did not want to come out as gay, because he would lose everything and everyone he loved: his family, his friends, his job as a minister, and his church. I felt a lump in my throat, because I knew that was the same thought process my son, Aiden, went through. Aiden lost his church and some friends, but did not lose his family. We all stood by him. Fortunately, Rev. Melvin also did not lose everyone and everything he loved.

After the event was over, people surrounded Bill. I stood in the outer circle, unsure of what I would say and how he would respond, but determined to introduce myself. I felt fairly confident that his presence at this event and his opening remarks signaled that he would be open to talking with me. But he did not know me. Would he think I was some weird mother? Would he see my passion as over the top for Japanese culture? I wasn't sure, but I had to try.

As people began to move away from Bill, I stepped closer. Then I was right in front of him. I shared that I was the mother of a transgender son and I wanted to do something for the Japanese American community to support, raise awareness, and build community for our *Nikkei* (Japanese American) LGBTQ+ individuals and families. He agreed to meet me for coffee.

When Bill and I met, he asked if there was a conference for *Nikkei* LGBTQ+ individuals and their families. I told him I was not aware of anything like that in the United States. In the end, we both agreed that a conference for families could be groundbreaking. I loved the idea, and with his support I decided to reach out to others I knew and set a meeting date.

If there was enough interest, maybe a small conference could be a great way to bring our Nikkei LGBTQ+ and allies together to learn, grow, and be in community.

I reached out to the Japanese American National Museum (JANM), The Aratani Foundation, and Rev. Mark Nakagawa from Centenary Methodist Church. When I met with Koji Sakai, Program Director at JANM, he offered to help us with free conference space. I met with Rev. Mark and he supported us wholeheartedly, offering free church space for our planning meetings in the early years of Okaeri. I approached Linda Aratani whom Aiden and I had met because she had come to hear us speak about our book, *Two Spirits, One Heart*, at JANM. The Aratani Foundation, which would later become a major donor for Okaeri, was not taking on new organizations to fund at that time. Linda, however, gave me a personal check for $2,500 which became the seed money for our first conference. More importantly, with the Aratani name, JANM,

Marsha & Aiden Aizumi, Linda & Sakaye Aratani

and Centenary's support, we had three respected Little Tokyo entities who we could show were supportive of our work. It was a beautiful start.

The next step was to gather individuals to discuss the idea of the conference. Koji gave us a meeting space at JANM. I invited about 12 people that I knew, but 18 people showed up, hearing about this new initiative. One of the people who heard about the meeting and showed up was Stephanie Nitahara, who was the Japanese American Citizens League (JACL) Regional Director for the Pacific Southwest. I wish I took a picture so I could name all who attended, but my memory is foggy now. I know Bill Watanabe was also there to support, as well as transgender activist Mia Yamamoto, Rev. Mark Nakagawa, and so many other wonderful supporters.

An ironic side story was that Stephanie had to leave early to meet her mother for lunch. At lunch, her mother said she was reading a book about a Japanese mother who has a transgender son. Stephanie then told her mother that she had just met with a Japanese mother with a trans son—they were both talking about me. Stephanie coming to the Okaeri meeting and connecting me with her mom led me to speak at the Christ Church of Chicago (Tri C). I often feel like there is a divine hand guiding me and others to find our way to each other.

Back to our first meeting, we discussed the idea of a conference and decided to move forward. We chose to focus on just the JA community so it wouldn't be too overwhelming for a first conference; plus, other Asian Pacific Islander (API) groups had their own spaces, so we wanted to keep it small and do it well. We were on our way. I was scared, but with the support of this small, passionate group I knew I was not alone. Aiden and our family felt so alone on our journey in the beginning. If this conference could bring comfort and hope to other families and *Nikkei* LGBTQ+ individuals, this felt like such an important thing to do for the community.

At our first meeting, we came up with a name—Okaeri. Okaeri means "welcome home" in Japanese, so we agreed this word would represent the work we were doing. One of our organizers, Eric Arimoto, who had left the JA community when he was 18, was encouraged by the thought of organizing this space for LGBTQ+ individuals like himself and his family. With varying experiences of being LGBTQ+ in the JA community, people were cautiously optimistic. But to be honest, there were those who were unsure how welcoming the space would be.

I understood that reluctance, because my family had also been met with different degrees of acceptance in JA spaces. Aiden was told by an older Japanese grandma (*obaachan*) with the sweetest voice that he was embarrassing our family by dressing so masculine, when he was identifying as a girl. Aiden said it took him a moment to realize he was being judged, because this *obaachan* was so polite. However, there were also JA family and friends who accepted my son with open arms.

In a way, I was surprised hearing this story from Aiden about that sweet JA grandma, because our community was discriminated against when the federal government put them in concentration camps during WW2. I thought, how could our JA *Issei* or *Nisei* individuals be so rejecting and judgmental, when their families were also judged and discriminated against? But it showed me that there was much work to be done, especially in undoing the mindset from WW2 incarceration that it was not good to stand out and be different, because being different makes people a target.

Yet, I was encouraged by the people who wanted to help create this conference. We could at least begin to have conversations that would bring greater understanding, awareness, and compassion to *Nikkei* LGBTQ+ individuals and their families.

I thought that if we could touch the lives of 100 people, that would be quite a feat. Since we had about 12 people helping to organize the conference, if each of us reached out to 10 people, perhaps we would have 100 individuals participating. It was a realistic goal. My fear of failure began to melt away.

For close to 18 months, this small group of organizers worked to create this space. riKu Matsuda was the first Okaeri co-chair with me. riKu brought an energy and hopeful heart that was infectious. traci ishigo was our first program chair, and Stephanie Nitahara was our first logistics chair. I oversaw finances and fundraising by default, but received a lot of fundraising support from others, especially Stephanie and her JACL connections.

On November 14 and 15, 2014, we held our first Okaeri conference at JANM. Over 200 people were in attendance. We kicked off Friday night with a film screening about a Japanese American from the LGBTQ+ community—George Takei and his documentary, *To Be Takei*.

Inaugural Okaeri Conference, 2014

The following day, we had a full schedule of plenaries and workshops. Dr. Greg Kimura, the CEO of JANM at the time, welcomed everyone to the space. Dr. Kimura shared privately with me that he had received pushback from some JANM members about why he was allowing an LGBTQ+ organization to hold a conference at the museum. We will always be grateful for Dr. Kimura standing up for Okaeri and making sure that we were supported and given visibility in this highly respected place.

The opening of the conference is a moment that is etched in my heart forever. Aiden and I were doing the next welcome after Dr. Kimura. I remember Aiden walking up the left side of the stage and I entered from the right. As he walked across the stage, he called out *"Tadaima"* which in Japanese means "I'm home" and is a greeting when you return from being away. As I walked from the other side to meet him I responded, *"Okaeri"* welcoming him home. My voice quivered and my eyes teared up. And I heard a few voices audibly exhaling with an "Awww" or "Ohhh" in response to this moment. It was all that we had hoped the name of the organization would mean—no matter how long or how far you had traveled from the JA community, you are able to return and be welcomed.

I don't remember what I said through my tears, but I do remember Aiden talking about this being the first time that he felt he was standing in front of a group of people, feeling they were seeing ALL of him. In JA spaces, he often felt like he had to hide being transgender, and in LGBTQ+ spaces, he felt embraced as LGBTQ+ but not always understood as a JA person. In that moment, he stood proud, knowing that he was being seen as his whole self. Okaeri changed his relationship with the JA community and allowed him to feel accepted in all of his identities.

As I began this journey of creating a Japanese American LGBTQ+ space, I didn't imagine it growing and bringing in others who wanted to make sure the space continued. After Okaeri 2014, this mighty group of volunteer organizers were exhausted and so we took a break to recuperate. What began as a one-time event seemed to have gained enough momentum to organize another conference in 2016. After some rest, this committed group began to meet again. Stan Yogi was my new Okaeri co-chair. Eric Arimoto, a steering committee member, wanted to focus on bringing back to the JA community more of the 40 and older, like himself, who left because they felt unwelcomed. That became the focus of our outreach in 2016, and another successful conference took place.

In 2018, for our 3rd biennial conference, a group of individuals led by Yasuko Sakamoto, Midori Dekura, Aya Tasaki, and Aya Yabe provided Japanese language conference programming, along with finding a team to translate a video called *A Love Letter*. *A Love Letter* was created and directed by Barney Cheng. Barney, a gay man, wanted to focus a film on two *Nikkei* families with transgender children.

Barney also filmed and edited the Okaeri Voices series, which is an ongoing project to capture the lives and thoughts of *Nikkei* LGBTQ+ individuals and allies over the age of 60. This is a project that was inspired by Gary Hayashi, a gay man, who wanted to make sure we did not lose these stories and history, and Gloria Fujita O'Brien, who was the lead organizer. We feel so fortunate to have captured stories such as Roy Kawasaki's, as he is no longer with us. Barney was able to show us not only Roy's journey, but also his beautiful soul. We also captured trailblazing parent Al Nakatani, who shared his story of losing all three of his sons, two of whom were gay. He turned his tragedy into a commitment to inspire parents to love their LGBTQ+ children. Al passed away in 2023, but his story will live on. His wife, Jane, continues to carry on their work through their organization, Honor Thy Children.

Okaeri Conference 2018

In 2019, Justin Kawaguchi became our newest co-chair and with him came a youthful vision for Okaeri. We entered the social media world. We also began to plan for Okaeri 2020, but due to the pandemic, we pivoted to virtual programming and postponed our conference to 2021.

Pivoting to virtual programming was a silver lining to this horrible wave of death that swept our country, because we could reach people around the United States and globally. We also started three support groups in 2020, known collectively as "Okaeri Connects!" One dedicated to the English speaking LGBTQ+ individuals, their parents, and allies, which kris mizutani helped to start, bringing in a network from Northern

California to support. There were also two separate Japanese speaking groups—one created by Aya Tasaki for LGBTQ+ individuals, and another created by Midori Dekura, Yasuko Sakamoto, and Aya Yabe for parents and allies. As of 2024, these three groups are still providing support, although the English speaking group has evolved into an LGBTQ+ closed group, with parents and allies being referred over to PFLAG San Gabriel Valley's API support group or PFLAG National's API virtual group.

In November 2021 with the pandemic still present, Okaeri held its 4th conference virtually. Over 300 people attended the 2 ½ day event. People joined from over 17 states and from foreign countries including Canada, Japan, Korea, Peru, and Singapore. We also hired our first part-time Okaeri staff: Cody Uyeda, our Program & Admin Coordinator, and Rino Kodama, our Tech & Media Marketing Coordinator. What began as temporary conference support positions has turned into permanent part-time positions, with both Cody and Rino still supporting Okaeri in 2024.

At Okaeri 2021, Friday began with a virtual speed meet-up, so people could get to know others. Saturday, we had an opening plenary and then people attended workshops and affinity groups we called "meetups." On Sunday, more workshops and meetups were available. The conference closed with a guest appearance by drag star, Gia Gunn, who shared her story as a trans woman, participated in a Q&A with her father, Carl Ichikawa, and closed the conference with a beautiful Japanese dance performance.

Throughout 2022, we continued to protect our community

from Covid through virtual programming such as a mental health workshop series, an Allyship Symposium, and continued commitment to our Okaeri Connects! support groups. And, we brought on a new co-chair, Mia Barnett, a passionate leader in the JA community.

Okaeri Conference 2023 Planning & Steering Committees

And that brings us to 2023: Ten years after our first meeting, 9 years after our first conference, and 5 years since our last in-person gathering. We held our first Okaeri Queer Obon in June 2023, drawing in over 400 people. We have been working on this book, *Letters to Home*, through most of this year. We have completed our 5th biennial conference, which was our largest endeavor to date. We added a virtual component, doubled our in-person workshop offerings, and developed more Japanese speaking spaces.

At Okaeri 2023, we had our first ever parent convening.

The parents created a Statement of Love and Commitment that was read at the conference. We ended Sunday with taiko drummers and Gia Gunn returning to lead an *Ondo* dance circle, which is a style of dancing performed during *Obon*. *Obon* is an annual Buddhist event commemorating one's ancestors and so we wanted to close our event by celebrating our queer and trans ancestors.

Our movement has grown and expanded to reach LGBTQ+ families, individuals, and allies in places we did not see in the beginning. We have visibility in Christian churches and Buddhist temples. We have Okaeri members in Northern California raising visibility, which began with the efforts of Kevin Mori, Stan Yogi, Christine Miyashiro, and tara u in partnership with the Japanese Cultural and Community Center of Northern California (The Center).

We are continuing to raise awareness of *Nikkei* LGBTQ+ issues with our connections to the Japanese American Citizens League (JACL), as well as local JACL chapters around the United States. And, our ties to Little Tokyo organizations such as the Little Tokyo Service Center, Japanese American National Museum, and Kizuna continue to grow.

Our efforts to create a home for the Greater Los Angeles Nikkei LGBTQ+ community have also resulted in other communities gravitating to us for support, resources, and connection. For many, the stigma of being LGBTQ+ has kept us feeling alone and ashamed. Okaeri has shown the JA community that the LGBTQ+ community can be successful if they are allowed to be their true selves. Our visibility and voice has reached people who may not have a community to belong to, especially through our virtual programs. More and more people are discovering that they are not alone.

Japanese and Japanese American LGBTQ+ individuals have always been a part of our community and families, but were often hidden. Okaeri has given these individuals the courage to step into the light because they see others who have done the same, been embraced, and loved. I believe if people know someone that is LGBTQ+, it makes it harder to hate and judge our community. As speaker and author Brene Brown says, "People are hard to hate close up. Move in."

I hope this book can be something that anyone can read, wherever you may live, and will give you a sense of the beauty, pride, challenges, and moments of achievement that live within our *Nikkei* LGBTQ+ community. I also hope you will read words from parents who love their LGBTQ+ children and share how their children's courage has opened their eyes to the richness and diversity in the world. With continuing homophobic and transphobic legislation, hate crimes, and hateful rhetoric being heard around the country, Okaeri wants this book to give you a glimpse of what moments of transformation, courage, hope, love, and joy can be.

My son, Aiden, is and has been a gift to me. My husband, Tad, and our other son, Stefen, have stood by Aiden and my advocacy work without question. Aiden has brought his wife, Mary, and Stefen has brought his partner, Cat, into our lives, and our family is closer than ever, living, loving, and respecting each other in deep and meaningful ways. Okaeri has been a gift to our whole family, because we now walk more openly and proudly, sharing our journey with others in the Japanese/Japanese American and API communities. We have thrown off our capes of invisibility and are showing others who we truly are. That process has been both frightening, and freeing at the same time.

Please read this book with a heart seeking to understand and learn. Thank you Michael Matsuno for your vision and passion to bring this book to fruition. Thank you to the amazing editing, design, and submission team of Daniel Tomita, Cody Uyeda, Rino Kodama, Kevin Mori and Michael once again. Thank you to all the writers and artists who have dared to step into a place of vulnerability. They are not all professional writers and artists, but people who have chosen to express something deep and personal with the world. May the words and art that they are sharing open a door to greater knowledge, compassion, and boldness in your life.

Okaeri is your community and we welcome you home.

WELCOMING

A LONG WELCOME

Nikiko Masumoto

You are welcome here.
You who are present
You who are trying to multitask
You who are powering through a hard day,
a hard week,
a hard year
You who are full of excitement and curiosity, and
you who carry the unknown and unsure
You who want to reach through the screen and hug someone
You who almost forgot to click on the link,
You are welcome.

You who are familiar, chosen family, strangers, new friends
and old, you are welcome.

You who come with dreams of dancing on summer nights
of sweat and sequins
of reaching your palms to the sky
was it in prayer or
getting down with your bad self or
reaching your palm to pick the perfect peach?
You who come with songs of love and liberation dancing
on your tongue
You are welcome.

You who come with enduring hearts
who are tired
who are missing someone
who have stood at the bedside
who have risen in the middle of the night
who have given the best care you could

You who have lost someone you love
You who have lost someone you never knew
You who are seeking renewal and connection
You who have given birth
You who are healers and *brujas*
You who are in need of rest or a vacation
You are welcome.

You who share roots
You who are queer in the country
You who are queer in the city
You who are melanin blessed

You whose grandparents or great grandparents loved
and lived from the land
You who know the scent of home by heart

You whose ancestors endured
whose ancestors survived
whose ancestors' lands were stolen
whose ancestors were forced to work on stolen land
You who have lost your ancestors
You who invite your ancestors home every year to dance *Obon
Odori* under swaying lanterns

You who come from lineages of workers and
dreamers and
makers and
stewards
You whose stories I have yet to learn

You who come with longing
You who come with offerings
You who come with joy!
You who work daily to make something special and meaning-
ful of your life
You who seek justice
You who keep hand-me-down recipes
You who are raising our children to love themselves
You who are seeking healing and relief
You who know failure
You who keep our kitchens full of our grandmothers' stories

You who bake pies and cookies and make preserves and
keep seeds and ferment vegetables and
You who wash our dishes and clean up our shit
You who I love fiercely
You who I do not yet know how to love
You and you
And you
You are welcome here.
You are welcome here.
You are welcome here.
We are welcome here.

FEET

Ellen Tanouye

I would like to focus on feet. Just plain feet. Since I am short, my feet are pretty puny. But they are what get me to the places I need to go. They can move at a pretty fast pace (especially on a tennis court!). Or they can move slowly, like a crawl. Mostly I am glad my feet allow me to be mobile, and I can stand strong, even if I am only 5 feet tall. Sometimes standing strong is not so easy. Our lives are filled with things that can knock us down. We may have financial worries. Or physical issues. We can have relationship challenges. We can feel overwhelmed by the daily news—earthquakes, war, mass murders. And there is always Covid. So just focusing on something tangible in plain sight can help us not to panic or give up. Just like our feet, we are here to put one foot in front of the other, even if we don't quite know what's ahead.

Eleven years ago, my partner Suzie was diagnosed with invasive, aggressive breast cancer. She was amazingly calm. And we relied on each other for support. Breast cancer is scary, and mastectomies and chemotherapy can be overwhelming. Yet we got through all the procedures and treatments, holding each other's hands (in a tight grip!) and hoping for the best. We had both come out of the closet just months before, so I was not so sure that our families would come alongside us and support us. They did not—both our families cut off relationships with us—but we were not surprised by their reaction. Who in the world would think that two women could be in a sustainable, healthy relationship at our ages? I was 60, and Suzie was 50, so we were not youngsters by any stretch of the imagination. Yet, Suzie and I had the courage and the determination to go through her cancer together, even if it was just the two of us.

We just put one foot in front of the other and kept going. It wasn't easy. It wasn't something we could navigate with confidence or assurance. But we didn't fall down. We stayed on our feet together. The love that we had for each other kept us strong and determined. And our feet, even though they are puny and weathered from age, kept us going. So, whenever we feel at a loss for what to do or how to proceed further, Suzie and I just look at our feet and see how far they have brought us, especially in being included and accepted by our families. Four years after they first cut off relations, the broken ties with our families started to be reconnected. It was a tentative, slow process, but today we are on good terms with both sides of our family.

We realize that sometimes our feet just need to be patient and step forward when the timing is right. No rushing. No stamping in impatience. One step at a time. And if our feet could tell the story, they would certainly say that no matter what, love is beyond all understanding and reason. Love is love. Our feet just know that.

CHRYSANTHEMUM PLAY

Dane Nakama

This series of ceramic works, titled "Boi Color," addresses the lesser known history of gay sex and a third gender (*wakashu*) of premodern Japan. Having previously considered their own queer identity as separate from their Japanese heritage, this body of work re-introduces themselves and others to sexually fluid aspects of Japanese history. The titles of the works were inspired by translations of medieval Japanese sex positions recorded in *Waka* poetry, and the forms embellished with *ukiyoe* masturbation diagrams and Sailor Moon memes. In particular, their piece titled "Chrysanthemum Play" is a translation of the term "*kiku asobi*," which was often used to describe anal play in premodern Japanese literature. The work has a *yakuza* tattoo pattern of a dragon tightly wrapped around an eggplant and

a tiger biting a peach—a subtle nod to how queer culture, like tattooing, has become a taboo subject in contemporary Japanese society.

The pot takes on a fleshy, torso-like appearance with bondage ties (*shibari*) wrapped and constricting the form. The piece is also accented by pages of BL (boys' love) manga tied in a Shinto wish tag fashion on the *shibari* cords, and a manga-inspired *omamori* (amulet) hanging from its flower arrangement—referencing the semi-religious origins of male on male sexual practices. With premodern Japanese history often presented in a reserved or regal context, these works share a more honest telling of history that allows members of the LGBTQ+ *Nikkei* community to recognize themselves in our own cultural histories.

3,000 YEAR BATH

Scott Oshima

Performed at QNA Eternal Spa on April 2, 2022 at the Geffen Contemporary at MOCA in Little Tokyo, CA.

Japanese bathing practices emerged from China and Korea around 1000 BCE. The practice traveled to Japan through Buddhism and flowed into Shinto *misogi* water purification rituals. The *Issei* carried the practice to America in the late 1800s. Many were single men living in boarding houses, hotels, and SROs without the luxury of baths. They would visit *sentō*—public baths—for a soak, a cleanse, a rest, and company—perhaps a friend or lover. Yet, unlike traditional communal *sentō*, some Japanese American versions were a single bathtub for rent in a solitary room. Little Tokyo alone was home to ten *sentō*, two of which were on the block where

Left: *Tokiwa-yu located inside the Takahashi Barber Shop. Courtesy of David Maldonado*

Bottom: *Illustration of sentō from first U.S. Naval expedition to Japan. Later censored because of mixed gender. Wilhelm Heine (1856). Archived in the Library of Congress Web Archives*

this performance took place: the Miyajima-yu and Tokiwa-yu.
Only the Tokiwa-yu's building still stands. Most *sentō* were
lost as a result of WWII Japanese American incarceration.

With help from my family, I took a bath in the ten *sentō* of
Little Tokyo, alone but not lonely.

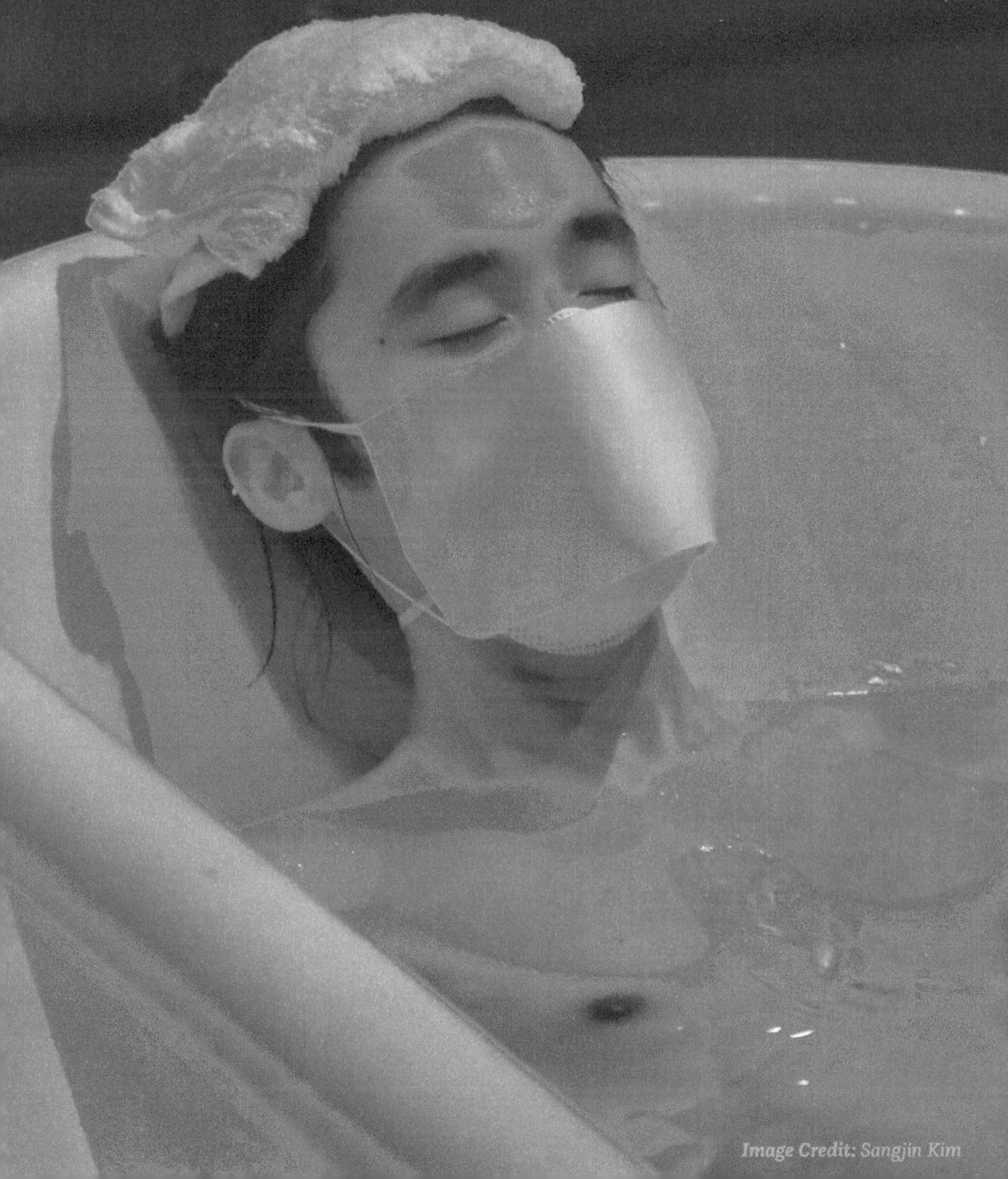

THINGS I THINK OF WHEN I THINK OF MY FATHER

Marilou Mariko Carrera

Part I

I visit the house you've lived in and loved for nearly thirty years.
I smile like I'm the parent, but not forgetting.

> Take a deep breath. Plant both feet on the ground. Feel the ground through the material of
> your shoes, socks, soles. If standing or sitting are not an option, lie down on your back and
> feel the ground through your spine.

I wonder about what it took to get you there –

things lost,

the ones left behind.

I see that you see them,

> As you are able, raise an arm in front of you, palm facing down. Extend.

just there,

as you stare vacantly out the kitchen window.

The roses flourish in the back,

their silky gestures attentive in the waning, evening sun.

Close your eyes for an extended moment. As you are able, raise the other above your head,
fingers spread wide.

How do we learn forgiveness?

Bae

Your mouth forms these shapes, BAH-ey.

would order you to go into the town by yourself at night,

you said.

In the mile of the shadows,

there and back,

bamboo whispered to your eight-year-old self.

Bring your hands back toward your core and curl your body into as tight a ball as you are able.

It was scary,

you said.

The sound of hauntings,

of darkness and *aswang* lullabies,

breathy and focused.

Reverse the tight ball and come to a neutral position. Take a few slow, deep breaths.

Why does this come back to me, this memory that is not my
memory?

You told me this to tell me you knew what it really felt like

to experience discrimination firsthand,

from the people you called family

even.

Extend a hand out to your family, chosen/kin, however you define. Change hands. Extend in
different directions, at different levels (above, to the side, below). Move between quick and
slow as it makes sense.

It felt like it was important to you,

though you said so little.

I hear the anguished cries of colonialism, imperialism, occupation,

centuries of violence;

Pause

and the angry protests of the direct

and also indirect

and also ill-defined impact of so many dictators' rules.

Gently make circles and semicircles with your neck. Reverse direction. Breathe. Stop after
three times in each direction or until you feel sleepy.

And underneath the cacophony,

the unspoken power of a child trying their best but not under-

standing,

not at first.

I hear this when I think of that bamboo language,

when I think of young you made to endure in that

shaky in-between time

after a war that wasn't yours,

after violence inherited

between two cultures you love (are)

and I love (am),

still.

Take a breath and release the tension. From the balls of your feet, bounce until you feel the motion in your chest, arms, and neck. Keep bouncing on one foot, and then the other, and back and forth a few times. Be quick.
Try being slow.

You weren't supposed to be there, yet there you were.

Their angry and frustrated words, wrapped in slurs,
found you, a child,
with Japanese blood, and also Filipino blood.
Unacceptable, unwelcome.

Close your eyes and *draw* a boundary around yourself. Breathe slowly until the line becomes a cool color that stays with you. Step out of the circle when you are ready, but not before. Open your eyes. Keep breathing.

The rough edges of their skin upon your still young skin,
one smack turned to more than one.
A nightmare you chose not to share when asked for a long,
long time.

Part II

Bae came to visit me while I was standing in a workshop
where I was asked to ask the ancestors to join me.

Make small circles with one arm. Make small circles with the other arm. Move them in the same direction at the same time. Change to moving them at different times. Change to bigger circles. And then bigger circles. Change direction. Pause.

She just appeared and didn't say a word —

Make circles above your head. Try circles on the side, behind, below you. Pause.

I mean, what is our language
except generations of skepticism and survival, adaptation
and resilience, deeply integrated in our touch and dance, our
colorful eats and fruits, our gatherings and care?

Twirl. Spin around, I mean. Repeat. Reverse. Until you are dizzy-ish, but still able to twirl.
Pause and consider the air that moves past when you are no longer twirling. Spinning
around, I mean.

I looked at her standing to my right side
and wondered if Bae was there to support or curse me.

Take in a deep breath. Open your mouth wide. Wider. Release the air. Release the sounds
trapped behind the air.

I felt confused and also afraid
(they come to me hand-in-hand, often)
and so I sat down and waited for the intense shame and sure enough,
it came.

Lie down and pull your legs close to your chest. Squeeze/Contract/Hug. Release. Sit up and
place your hands on your pelvis, anchoring your thumbs behind your hip bones. Squeeze/
Contract/Hug. Release. Place your hands on the opposite shoulders. Squeeze/Contract/Hug.
Release into the space. Repeat. Repeat. Repeat.

Body holding these bodies of truth.

Isn't it true I want to connect and also to reclaim?

Find a new shape. Find a new shape that makes you feel grounded, comforted. Keep trying
new shapes until you get closer to this feeling. Take a breath with each shape.

Part III

A tender body emerges,
wondering if there is enough love to spare
for a late body,

Place your hand on your heart and feel for rhythm, moving through the seasons and ache and
joy and repair.

a wandering body,

Soften your gaze or close your eyes and call up the last place you sought pleasure, yourself.

a body being forgotten,

Place your other hand onto your forehead, cupping the memories, ask them if they are real.

yet encountering the embrace of
full lips, full hips,
soft tips of fingers searching my neck, back,
grip the tightness of these once fierce hamstrings,
while I ride the waves of those I was told I should not want,
but wanting and finding a home in
scents of honey and sour and wet grass after a spring rain.

I open, slowly.

Become slow.

I usually start with my breath.

Become air.

I massage my calves and thighs.

Become body.

I stare at my nose under a bright light.

Become mountain.

I open my mouth and risk connection with practiced, intentional sounds.

Become opening.

I listen for sentimentality in music and try to find myself there.

Become vibration.

I sit in uncertainty with an arrhythmic pulse I think must be love and curiosity.

Become warm electric glow.

Maybe it's only that for now, I proceed with care.

Keep going. Pause. Resume. Repeat. Reverse. Resolve. Reconsider. Rest. Remind. Relearn. Slow. Breathe. Slower.

i. WELCOMING

garden, community is what we build.

02

THE EARTH AND THE BODY

SURIPPA/スリッパ

kris mizutani

Some soft
Some with cushioned heels

Others with tatami insoles
Like my bed, they are home

More than feet warmers
They are the layer

Between the earth and me
The boundary between outside and in

I turn them around in pairs
Ready for my return home

藍色
kris mizutani

I am the richest blue you can imagine.
Earthy but also celestial.

When you see me, there is a calm that washes over you.
My depths are unseen, yet I bring about serenity.
When you see me, you want to rest and be held.

I am often used for tie dyes, because of the beautiful contrast I provide.
If I were a person, I'd be described as grounded, wise, and content.

I am also the color of deep sky and oceans.
This isn't a coincidence.

Stars shine bright against me.
Even though I'm in the background, life isn't rendered visible
without me.

BECAUSE OUR ROOTS FIND EACH OTHER UNDERGROUND

anaïs peterson

because

> sunflowers keep coming up, first growing
> against the worn lattice of my front porch on
> a sticky august afternoon, then cut and sold
> from leaking black bins at sunday morning
> farmers market in boston, shocking me bright
> and blooming between the cracks in the cement
> inside the walls of a pennsylvania state prison,
> and finally on a thursday afternoon in march
> where she describes us as perfectly arranged
> sunflowers, catching the long rays of sun in an
> infinite moment of long novels and naivety.

because the world ends and begins and ends and ends

because our world is small and the head of a sunflower is not
one flower but a thousand tiny blooms

because i am grown from rain-soaked illinois soil, sunlight
peeking out from wispy gray skies and the way you say my
name a's softer than a whisper during sunday sermons—
the smallest joys of living

because sometimes, when i laugh, your giggle slips out and lingers
on the air, stirring up courage in my soul whispering softly
i am still with you even when they can not see me, you have
never been the only one

because sunflowers will always turn to find the sun

because the sun is the sound of a smile catching on your lips
when you say my name and the glimmer in your eye when
you smile only at me

because in every variation we find our way back to sand between
our toes, garden plots in the backyard, to dark blue waves
glimmering with the longs rays of the sun and glowing pink
with evening clouds gently landing on the shore

because a sunflower without deep roots will fall back to earth,
exhausted by the weight of carrying the flower

because standing in your kitchen i could close my eyes and be in
my aunt's house with coffee brewing on the black countertop
or in the small kitchen of my childhood home pots piled up
in the sink my dad taking leftovers out of the fridge for lunch

because the further a sunflower's roots spread the taller they
grow, sturdy green stems and striking yellows flowers reaching
out to the sky

because you remind me we live in the same world as a field

blue with scilla blooms, of small dandelions woven in my
hair, of tight hugs that steal my breath, and of moments
where we hold each other with the love we have always
given away
because planting sunflowers too close together results in
weak stems and toppling stalks but plant them in the
same field and their roots will find each other underground working together to heal the soil

FREESIA

Ian Martyn

When I was young, my *Nisei* grandmother introduced me to the joys of gardening. I would often visit her at my aunt's house where the backyard became the stage for our planting escapades. One of my favorite things in those early days of my life was the bulb and the various different forms in which they came. We started by populating one of the planting beds with freesia corms she had bought for me. One of the first things I remember my grandmother saying about bulb plants is that they would appear each spring, burst into impressive bloom, then die back. They weren't truly dead, however; under the soil the bulb itself stayed hidden, guarding water and nutrients in its body to survive the cold winter and burst forth the next year with the same impressive display.

One could say that the bulb is simply hiding under

the soil, but indeed it never stops working. The bulb constantly manufactures nutrients for itself, delighting in its rejuvenation each year while also cultivating its hidden self. Indeed, one of the many impressive properties of the bulb is its ability to reproduce under the soil, building community wherever it exists. This property allows it to spread both above and below the ground.

I think of my grandmother's own struggles throughout her life. Her journey took her from her birthplace of Portland to Los Angeles after her family lost their land, then to Rohwer incarceration camp in Arkansas during WWII, then to Chicago post-incarceration, and finally back to Los Angeles. After each metaphorical winter of forced movement, she would reappear in a display of color. She grew not only herself but her community of both family and peers, and I consider myself lucky to have been a part of her community.

Examining my grandmother's life through the lens of a bulb allows me to think about how community grows and develops over time, starting small but growing into something larger throughout the years. When I reflect about the meaning of community, I think of these bulbs and their extraordinary lives. While they may not always be visible, they are always working, multiplying in close proximity to nurture and grow their communities. While they may have brilliant displays above ground for all to see, the real magic happens under the surface, a world only known by the bulbs themselves. Likewise, although we build community to be visible and show what we can do, the most important aspects often revolve around the hidden work we do for ourselves and our peers, creating comfort in the community that we've built where we can share secrets that only we understand.

Like my grandmother showed me in the garden, community is what we build. Whenever I find myself getting tired or needing to retreat to solitude, I often think of the bulb's steady yet tireless effort to keep going, and I remember those early days of my life spent with my grandmother in the garden, the freesias we planted blooming just a bit more each year until the entire bed would burst into a vibrant display of color.

TADAIMA

Anne Watanabe

and the snake pit would say back to
me: *okaerinasai.* each night sleeping
on the edge of a knife. the
warmest mouth: mouth full of teeth.

so allergic to the smell of home
it made me choke   stuffed
white men in my cunt
to shut her up

she was on the verge of toxic shock
by the time i find you, yelling in your ear
at the bar   about being *yonsei*
do you like being Japanese?

    somehow she creaks open
at last. crocodile teeth arched tight
around the skin of my desire

still she hangs open in a yawn
rusted hinge
                grating
ready to slam
              but opening

       we came from a culture   where families never say
       "i love you"   never hug   never touch
        unless they have to.   it seems impossible
        for two souls like ours to meet   let alone touch
                      let alone exist

I couldn't look you in the eye
a century slipped by between us

  and still
we recognize
      each other

when we were seeds inside seeds
we crossed each other   in the ocean:
hiroshima to vancouver   okinawa to hawai'i

so many times we left home for another home
            so we could meet in a city

             with no trace of ancestors
but my cunt is an old witch that cannot stop telling the truth
she called me here:

where lake michigan licks my feet
                    to stick them to this sand.

where sharp teeth   and rusted hinge   hold this heart
                             & cunt
     the truth pours out
       & we drink together.

COFFIN, 2042

Anne Watanabe

in the future where you lived,

I'm holding the phone to my ear on
father's day. i never send a card but

sometimes, i text. *happy 58th birthday.*
hope you have a great day. you try so hard

to love me and i try not to repeat
your mistakes. you build the muscle

of *i'm sorry.* say it a dozen more times
before you die. 1.5 times for every

two years of my childhood. you almost
say   things would have been different

for you   if you were born today.

I finally say *I love you.* the words no longer
sour old food being flossed out of teeth.

more like   baby tooth that waited years
for its turn   finally falling out at last

       in its 33rd year.
step eight: made a list of all persons we had harmed,

and became willing to make amends to them all. step
nine: made direct amends to such people wherever

possible
when we eat sushi in toronto   i wince

at your bad jokes. we fight about
abolition   but i still take you to your first

protest against prisons. fingers get cold
holding signs   and you don't do

chants but you stay til the end. *that was*
very interesting. but you know   there are

some really bad people in there.
we visit tashme together one

day. don't say much   but i wonder
if you can tell it's a prison.   if it reminds you

of days when you looked forward to ramen
cheetos and hot water   in a bag. or if you can

imagine   in eighty years our descendents
might pilgrimage   to curran-fromhold

correctional facility   and there's nothing left
                         but a museum

                       but it's 2012   i'm shuffling papers
                 found in your apartment: recipes for *gyoza*
                  wrinkled with dried water. with no wife to
                  make them for you,   did
              you get a chance to fold   those plump pockets
                   of home   before your heart stopped?

in the future where you lived, it's 2042
and you still die in the end   but

i'm holding your wrinkled hand
on your deathbed.   singing to you

as morphine falls in the drip chamber.   while i nurse
the grief that finally   had a chance
                              to grow up.

FINDING AUTHENTICITY AS A QUEER, NIKKEI DANCER

Gabrielle Kazuko Nomura Gainor

Growing up, I was taught that when I return home, I call out *"Tadaima!"* to my family inside the house. Those who respond with *"Okaeri"* ("Welcome home!") are not simply living family members, but ancestors, too. As a dancer/ choreographer, I strive to honor my ancestors and my community by creating works that make us feel seen and represented.

The following images are of a dance piece I choreographed titled *in the beginning, woman was the sun*, a queer Asian reimagining of Shinto mythology. This performance wove together contemporary ballet and traditional Japanese dance to tell a story of the Shinto sun and moon deities, *Amaterasu* and *Tsukuyomi*, and their break-up—which led to the creation of night and day. Ultimately, *Amaterasu* (the sun) comes out on top, and *Tsukuyomi* (the moon) is pushed out of her orbit—forced to follow her across the sky for all eternity.

My collaborator and friend, Truong Nguyen, a gay, first-generation Vietnamese American, performed as the sun goddess *Amaterasu*. And I, a queer Japanese Filipina American, performed as the moon god, *Tsukuyomi*. These characters allowed us to bring forth parts of ourselves that are not always accepted in daily life. I grew up socialized as a girl and trained in ballet—an art form with rigidly heteronormative gender roles. But playing *Tsukuyomi* allowed me to explore what it feels like beyond these narrow definitions of womanhood and femininity. I imagined that I was Rufio from *Hook*, Oberon from *A Midsummer Night's Dream*, and Jareth from *The Labyrinth*. I breathed in—feeling what it's like to have a body that has no obligation to be thin or pretty—yet can

move in a way that commands peoples' attention when I'm on stage. I realized that the freedom I experienced through this character is always mine to return to. Gender is a dance of its own to be enjoyed and reinvented—never an obligation to keep doing the same routine again and again.

After creating this dance, I learned that various Shinto

deities could be
interpreted as LGBTQ+:
the expansive *Inari
Okami* (sometimes
portrayed as a man,
sometimes as a
woman, sometimes as
encompassing multiple
genders), or the sun
goddess *Amaterasu*
(depending on one's
interpretation of the
cave myth, she is seen
as having same-sex attraction in that particular story).

When queer *Nikkei* carve out space for ourselves within Japanese culture or traditions, we're not trying to dilute or distort the culture. We have so much love for where we come from, and just want to feel authentic in every way. When we proudly share our stories as queer *Nikkei*, we are like "the self that has to invent and create" in order to thrive, as Bell Hooks described.

A video of in the beginning woman was the sun, *performed live at Seattle's Erickson Theatre can be viewed at gabriellekazuko.com or via the QR code to the left.*

EVERY BODY HAS A STORY

Keila Sachi Gaballo

おかえり(*okaeri*), to me, especially in relation to identity, speaks to my time educating myself around trauma-informed somatic practices and research. *Okaeri* speaks to being greeted back into my body. I think it is even more powerful than ただいま (*tadaima*) or "I'm home, I'm back, I have returned," because *okaeri* is a WELCOMING—it is communal, just as the process of healing should be.

This piece that I painted represents a homecoming to my ancestors, our cultural and earthly roots, and most of all, a welcoming home from my truest and core sense of self or spirit. I always say, "every BODY has a story," and this piece is a nod to that along with the saying "we are all walking libraries." We hold not only our own stories, but the stories of our ancestors as well. Returning home to my body has been like slowly cracking open the stories within me and slowly feeling more empowered to connect with the narratives living inside me.

I created this illustrative self portrait on a 41 x 24 inch birchwood board with acrylic ink, acrylic paint, colored pencil, water-soluble crayon, and sumi ink. I then edited the image digitally to add more texture, depth, and color. I enjoy working in mixed media because I feel it best represents me as someone with a fluid racial, gender, sexual, and disabled identity. I am able to play with each medium individually, but also draw connections to the intersectionality of my own identities by allowing the interaction of each medium to highlight the beauty in each layer.

I worked entirely outdoors and engaged in several different somatic and embodiment practices which helped shape the final piece. The natural elements inspired me to use a wooden board as my canvas.

Throughout this illustration, you will find aspects of my *Ryukyuan* (*Shimanchu*), *Ainu,* and Japanese culture in the *hajichi* (tattoo) elements on their hands and butterfly, the *bingata* inspired floral design in their hair, and the use of sumi ink to outline and create movement. Growing up I often felt insecure about my body (my height, my figure, and skin color) so I highlighted these aspects of myself in the illustration. The process of creating this art piece was incredibly healing and allowed me to feel even more at home in my body. I felt a sort of comfort and confidence that I have not experienced before, and since completing this painting, I have been able to explore more of what makes up my identity

as a queer, disabled, indigenous artist.

The diasporic community I have found online with my *choodee* (*Uchinaaguchi* [Okinawan language] word for "family") over the past few years has provided such a special and meaningful connection. They have not only given me a sense of belonging and a safe space to grow, learn, and heal, but they have also helped me find new meaning in

my passions, identity, and purpose. They have allowed me
to feel safe enough to embrace my own fluidity, queerness,
neurodivergence, and disability, which also helped me create
spaces that allow others to feel empowered to do the same.

03
八方美人
THINGS
siblings
integrity
sexuality
materiality
vilege/s
taste
envy
sex
leases
contracts
deadlines
relationships
hot
BUT AT LEAST SHE SAW
TO ME, MEAN

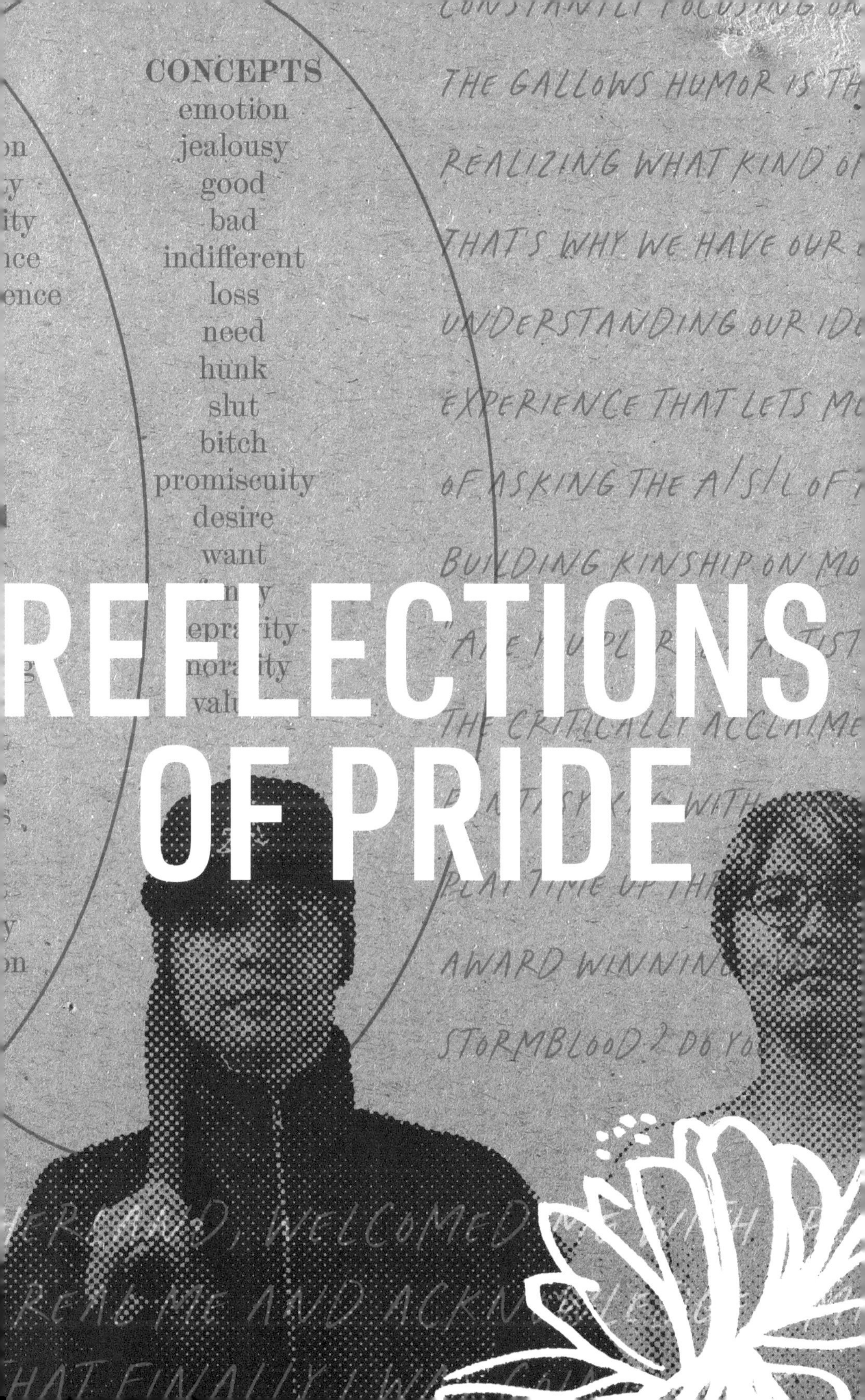

CONCEPTS
emotion
jealousy
good
bad
indifferent
loss
need
hunk
slut
bitch
promiscuity
desire
want
epravity
norality
valu

REFLECTIONS OF PRIDE

WHAT IS PRIDE?

Aiden Aizumi

Pride is love.
It is lifting each other up, standing together, crying together,
celebrating together.

Pride is a revolution.
It is showing the beauty in our differences, letting our
intersections shine.

Pride is anger.
It is the collective pain we feel when trans women of color are
taken too soon. It is the fire in our bellies to fight for justice in
their names.

Pride is a riot.
It is honoring the history of the movement. It is honoring
the lives of Marsha P. Johnson and Sylvia Rivera who helped
us pave the way. It is our continued fight to be seen as equal,
valid, and respected.

Pride is resilience.
It is being told over and over that our lives are not as valuable.
It is standing up again and again despite acts of violence,
anti-LGBTQ+ laws, lack of healthcare, job discrimination, and
housing discrimination.

Pride is hope.
Hope that we continue to overcome. Hope for tomorrow.
Hope that one day, our lives as LGBTQ+ people will be seen
for how wonderful they are.

Pride is power.
It is knowing our stories, experiences, and lives are powerful
tools for changing the world.

Pride is visibility.
It is true representation of the LGBTQ+ community. It is
inclusive. It is diverse. It is not white-centered.

Pride is solidarity.
It is standing up and speaking out. It is a call to stand with
Black Lives Matter and all struggles against racism.

Pride is expression.
It is strutting down the street, feeling fine and looking fabulous. It is the freedom to live and exist just as we are, because who we are is beautiful.

Pride is me.
It is waking up every day to face the world authentically as a queer, trans, Japanese American man. It is holding true to myself. It is being visible for the next generation of LGBTQ+ folks. It is honoring where we have been and knowing how much further we need to go, and hoping my story, voice, life, will somehow contribute to that progress.

SHARED EXPERIENCE IS A HELLUVA DRUG

Tomo Hirai

Content warning: hate, mass casualty events, gun violence, Japanese wartime incarceration.

When you're Japanese American, there's one inescapable question that eventually comes up no matter what setting you're in. "Where was your family sent to during the war?" It's a source of instant camaraderie, and sometimes a shortcut for understanding where you're from or who you are. But what about the people whose family did not go to camp?

Your family's wartime experience becomes something like a closeted identity, something you stay away from unless people pry. And when they do, you have to—almost apologetically—admit, "actually my family never went to camp."

When Ryan Yamamoto, a KPIX 5 CBS News anchor in San Francisco, spoke about his family experience, he admitted feeling left out from those conversations because his father's family had elected to "voluntarily" evacuate out of California to Utah, avoiding the wartime concentration camp experience (though they faced their own hardships while "free").

Similarly, if you're from the San Francisco Japanese American community, there's another distinct shared experience of living through Redevelopment, which wrote off the ethnic enclave as "blighted" and rebuilt the community into a tourism-dependent shopping mall.

While deeply traumatic, these experiences help tie people together and forge a sense of community. Sharing in these experiences helps define what it traditionally means to be Japanese American in San Francisco.

Yet I'm none of these. On my mother's side, my grandmother worked in a factory making airplane propellers during the war while my grandfather worked as a doctor in Osaka. On my father's side, my grandmother stayed home to look after the family business while my grandfather went off to fight in the Philippines. My family stories about the war are about surviving air raids and the starvation they faced during the occupation years.

People often ask me, "Hirai, that's not a name you hear a lot. Are you related to that San Francisco State professor?" And no, I have no family in the United States aside from my parents who immigrated here in the early 1980s. I am a newcomer and an outsider in the Japanese American community, and can understand that feeling of being left out that Yamamoto spoke of.

I have a Japanese face, but not the traditional connections. I know the history and gravity, but have no personal skin in the game. I feel like I should belong, but I am an outsider looking in.

To me, the shared experience of being queer is what gives me a sense of community. Instead of asking "which camp?", I cultivate my circles based on questions like, "where did you migrate to after Elon took over Twitter?" It's the shared sense of trauma and hurt that makes everyone relatable and understanding of what we're going through. Thus, only in queer spaces can I feel comfortable in bringing my whole self without fear.

For so many years, I never felt like I fit in with the Japanese American community because my whole self didn't have that place. Even now, I bring a version of myself that's "presentable" to the community and befitting of the soft-spoken, intelligent and capable trans woman people wish me to be. In reality, I am far from it. I am a dissociative mess who feels more kinship with cats than people, a so-called Casanova with half a dozen girlfriends—four of them pink-haired vtubers streaming on twitch.tv—and "terminally online." I'm a messy piece of work, is what I'm saying.

I have a cishet friend. She and I meet for lunch or dinner on occasion. She likes to ask me, "how do you do it? How do you manage having four five seven girlfriends?"

I shrug. I don't know. I love them and they love me. They know I'm exhausted, and I know they're exhausted. We watch anime and play video games together and dream of one day having enough money to buy a house so we can all live together instead of over four different U.S. States, Canada, Brazil and Iceland. It's a deep, mutual connection, like one formed through prisoners being marched to the firing squad together.

I can't bring that sense of self and gallows humor to anyone outside. I once told a group, "I honestly didn't think I'd live past 30," (I'm 35 now, by the way) and the reaction was shock and pain.

"That's really sad," one person in the Japanese American community once said to me.

Of course it's sad. But that's not why I said it.

My resignation over probably being dead at 30 stemmed from years of growing up under the specter of Christian fundamentalism taking hold in the Bush years, having trans rights left out in favor of focusing on gay marriage, and the constant backlash against queer people that has only seemed to grow in tenor since 2015. Sure, things have "gotten better," but if what's "better" is a society that reminds me daily that political forces are trying to legislate me out of existence, I can't help but think it's not that much better. Having lived five years past my expected expiration date, it's now more like a delayed fate, one rescheduled to a date TBD. So while I blew past my "deadline," I'm now instead constantly haunted by the thought that I will die Soon™.

So when I say I expect an early death, it's more in line with the Japanese phrase: "Shikata ga nai." "It is what it is." I'm not looking for pity so much as I'm stating a reality and a wish for something better. It's like saying "it's hot" during a 100+ degree heatwave or "we need the rain" during a multi-year drought.

In my experience, when I express these depressing feelings, I elicit pity from most people because I deserve better, and I do. But while that allyship is well-meant and appreciated, it doesn't necessarily forge a bond with me. Many people, including romantic partners, have said they'd fight for me, but the concept of fighting—being willing to take a bullet for me when the time comes—isn't necessarily the sacrifice I'm asking for, nor expect. What I look for when I say things like this is kinship rather than resources, because this isn't about activism, or doing what's right, but plain-old daily survival.

Constantly focusing on survival is exhausting. The gallows humor is there to soften the blow of realizing what kind of reality we live in. That's why we have our own shortcuts to understanding our identities. It's shared experience that lets me skip the pleasantries of asking the A/S/L of traumas we've borne by building kinship on more fertile ground.

"Are you plural? Autistic? A furry? Do you play the critically acclaimed MMORPG Final Fantasy XIV, with a free trial with unlimited play time up through level 70, including the award winning expansions Heavensward and Stormblood? Do you like weed?"

These are the questions that help build rapport among ourselves as queers and are part of our identity that matters to us now. We cut through to the simplest and lowest bar of entry: "what camp was your family in?"

So when I speak to someone as not only a queer person, but a Japanese American queer person, I have difficulty in being able to click. My "fitting in" within the community is challenged by not only my queerness, but my family history that removes me from the common experience of Japanese Americans on the West Coast. It's perhaps why I get along better with other *Shin-Nisei* or queers like myself, and why that connection feels so much more instant and solid when it's both.

The saying goes, "take a walk in someone else's shoes," but the shoes alone are never the full experience. Just as I will never be able to truly understand the intergenerational trauma and anger of the wartime incarceration, I can pour my soul out to evoke sympathy and understanding from others, but it's nothing like the empathy felt from shared experience.

A VAGABOND'S LIFE (WITHOUT THE ROMANCE): A POLEMIC ON THE MEANING OF HOME

Wayne Itoga

I am conventionally single-family housed. From an urban planning POV, an extravagant resource-guzzling blight on the landscape. It's expensive. A bank owns my home (mortgage) and can evict me (foreclose) if I don't pay my rent (mortgage payment). I'll be 80 something when my mortgage is paid off and I'm looking forward to the extra pocket money and the time I'll have to enjoy it. Looking back over what I guesstimate to be about the last two-thirds of my life, I've never lived in any one place for more than ten years, and in some spots, considerably less. It's ironic given how much I hate change. But here I am in that spot, just about a year shy of becoming my longest stay anywhere.

My house is unsettled. Books stacked in two or three foot towers waiting to topple. A living room full of unpacked moving boxes, symbolic I think. One of my parents died when I was a child. I was left for another man in my early 40s. I am deeply scarred and embark on any enterprise requiring more than a silent nod with caution. Trepidation, suspicion, fear. Resistance. Two or three in the hand and more than five in a kitchen drawer and some more stashed in the garage are worth more than...

I don't know what it means to be home in an emotional sense. I am not secure. I understand home as an external place, a state, not a feeling. Something outside of me like bell bottoms or hoop skirts. I've never felt the physical rush or visceral connection to a place that has announced to me that I'm home. Permanence and possibility is a rotator cuff injury—that's inside, I understand that. In an occasional flickering wink of awakening, I understand that our worldly existence can't offer me that kind of security, doesn't owe it to me, that it's a selfish desperate need—and in an even lesser fractional fleeting fly-speck of enlightenment, I'm not sad about it. It's simply what IS and there's never anything good or bad about what IS. IS is neutral. IS is balanced. WTF? Yep, it's a crazy world and IS is a condition of living in it. Not so hard right? There are a lot harder things to accept and understand: what goes on in a boyfriend's mind (let's explore that one some more!); how a billionaire could want more and eliminate existing jobs to get it (let's explore that one some more!); cruelty, unkindness, prescription drugs. I lied just now and enjoyed it—it's all the unfathomable same! As long as we're in love with life, we're stuck with it—what IS.

Me—I'm like a magnet ever attaching to more worldly

goods, more material possessions that stand-in for things: love, beauty, stability, affirmation, visibility, audibility, things that change! Things that can't be held or dominated or controlled. Things that are the very nature of this impermanent life. I think about how far the jump from understanding in the head is to living something in the heart.

DISQUISITION.

I think there was a perfume called Samsara. It's like naming a brand of corn chips Obesity. Samsara is the corrupt earthly delusional world that only serves to keep us bound to the source of all our suffering and misery.

The corollary/symbiotic/parasitic relationship, not the opposite, is Nirvana; not a conscious sensate heavenly paradise, but nothing. Cessation. A state where ALL our earthly notions cease. No white light, no other side, no crossing over, no baseball, fireworks, opera, or classical ballet (the four fundamental building blocks of all life!). No robocalls, scams, influencers, monetization. No re-unions, celestial choirs. No competition, jealousy, envy, money, life, death. Cessation. Nothingness. Non-existence. That is one heavy God-damned trip.

In my adolescence, I spent a lot of time in a friend's home. It wasn't perfect or without visible obvious dysfunction, but it was loving and stable and stimulating and inclusive, but I always knew it wasn't my home. I spent time in my aunt's home as well, which happened to be across the street from a home my father rented for a time. It wasn't perfect and very much dysfunctional, but I also found the love I needed there for a time. I stayed with a second cousin too while I was relocating for college. I didn't name it at the time, but what was indelibly impressed on me was conditionality. I also wondered if passive-aggressive was in the maternal side's DNA. I learned that blood is thick and sticky. The status of the guest. The profundity of being a stranger in an intimately familiar land. I think I began thinking of myself as a vagabond somewhere around this time, a wanderer with no permanent mooring—not with that sophistication certainly, but feeling alien. Desperate to belong. It was a time for nurturing the insecurities that I would spend the next 45 years finding buried like landmines or mummies, stupidly surprised, trying to disarm them without losing a piece of mind or a chunk of heart, rifling through the wrappings to find the protective amulets and jewels.

At that time in my life, "found family" was not a term making the rounds and the families that I did find could not provide me with their home, could not financially nor emotionally rescue, sustain, or heal me. They can and did offer, and open-handedly give me, an extravagant array of things, but there were limits to what I could ASK for, of, what could be offered I think. What I got was not always what I wanted, what I needed. Terrible conundrum, no? The guilt of receiving expressions of kindness and love. How much of a burden can a family member be asked or expected to pick up and carry? Do you test such unspoken/assumed formulae? I understand "found/chosen family" intellectually, but I don't have the guts to believe in it.

Being Asian, gay, petite, pimpled, unstylish, uncool, a product of the seminal AIDS generation, self-hating, and closeted produced in me an alphabet soup of neuroses feeding like bacteria on my streak plate of insecurities. Fortunately at the time, I was spared (or spared myself) the self-knowledge that I didn't belong in the mainstream world of my gay white peers (why is a jury of a presumed whatever so unlike the whatever?). I was about as far from being a clone as you could get and I certainly couldn't pass. I didn't have information. I didn't have the alligator polo, the button fly Levis, or the white sneakers. More significantly, I didn't have any me. I couldn't Google anything. I was afraid. I couldn't dance. I didn't bar. I didn't fuck. I couldn't swim. So I grabbed the side and took the long way round, never just cutting right across to what I saw, what I wanted. Given the stats, I can't regret it, and given my all or nothing personality, I'd no doubt be dead, but negation is its own kind of death. Independence is its own unique mythology, but you do learn to cope and do without; it's just that when you do it like that, by yourself in that awful silence—it's crippling. Community is radically different depending on what you look like and acceptance in any community is hugely predicated on that. In my gay-certain sexual identity-forming days, almost no one in visible culture, queer or otherwise, looked like me—not enough to gain traction anyway. No leading men, no porn stars, no models, no athletes; and along with them, I too was invisible—though when I finally learned about Bruce Lee I had some major whack fests. I was 40 when I finally had sex with an Asian man ([Glen] not disappointing); in introspect, the major milestone in a long journey to self-acceptance. 40. Those are the cookie cutters that have shaped how I see, how I understand identity, home, family, belonging, love, relationships, attraction, sex—the awesome cockeyed beautiful blazing litany of life.

Home is a loaded word, inextricably bound up with nostalgia and innocence for a good clod of us; notions of an 'irrealized' idealized ether-world for me. Like my relationship to food, a parade float, a bridal gown, baptisms, Christmas trees; things all loaded with ideas and concepts that transcend purpose, survival, and the need to eat. To be emotionally or literally homeless is to be othered, un-grounded; marginalized and outcast if you talk too much too often and too long about it. Like being divorced or worse: single, childless, fat, unemployed, under-employed, disabled, sexual, adulterous, promiscuous. Words that are privileged, subjective, and cis-conventionally judgmental. The social compact is expensive, exclusive, and limiting. To be homeless is seen as a moral failing, a fault not taking into account illness, poverty, capacity—context. You're unintentionally but necessarily subversive, and on many many levels, threatening.

For my suburban class, home is where I learned the most about a lot of real basic things—the early childhood-acquired ideas and feelings that underpin lifelong adult emotions. How we do or don't communicate. Our need for or inability to give/accept affection—affection here synonymous with compliments (please think about it). Those crucial years before mixing with other kids, the nascent knowledge that there are Other People. Hearing and seeing Others on a consistent basis changes everything. The learned stupidity, prejudice, ingesting ignorance—adding to your own, ugh, what a rich stew. I think it's different now because in a two-parent household, both are more likely to work, but in my suburban lab in the waning years of *Father Knows Best*, you spent a huge gob of time with One Teacher. Genetic markers nurtured into behaviors; amplified, squelched, shaped, spanked, inhibited, subsumed, sublimated, suppressed, all before the conscious power of choice. Without autonomy, without freedom, exceptionally discussed but mostly ordered, conformed. On that empty stage, without maturity, self-obsession not self-reflection, the great sad detour of self-immolating rebellion; the intervention of wisdom and compassion from your adult brain still many years and experiences in the future.

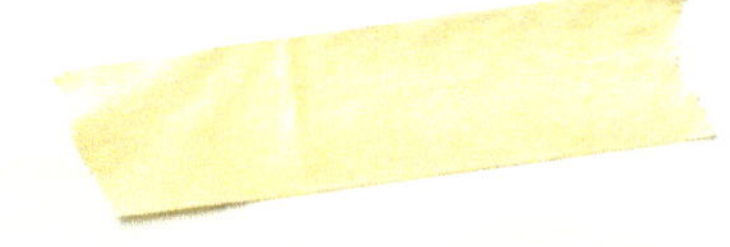

I see home as a quasi-fantasy, an operatic spectacle we're drawn to by comforts that were neither earned, appreciated, nor accurate; the labor, expense, heartache-break and feelings of providers, major parts taken by other actors, rarely recalled by the memoirist. The need to rationalize/reinvent and the power to distort are very great and very old friends.

Home physically contains The Family, and so family

shapes, influences, determines a gigantic part of who we are; it doesn't shape dementia or stomach cancer but it does shape how we interact with other people and how we interpret and inhabit our world. And I think this is what we mean when we talk of home, and with distance, figure out what we got or didn't get, and who we are because of it. The Family: ma and pa, same sex, non-nuclear, raised by grandparents, wolves, an endless permutation, but conceived in the popular consciousness as something on TV. Endless boxcars added to our train that, if we're lucky, we learn that we can, and what to, decouple. That it matters what we want. The past is obviously important but it's not really us—it's habit and comfort and complacency, scabs or scars, siblings, rivalry, popularity, envy, disappointments, failings—but it does not have to define and control who we are, right now. Here. Today. I think we cling to a mythic home because it improves with age and in contrast, the now only offers uncertainty. The now is changing/destabilizing, unreliable, subjective, contextual, privileged, biased, and infinitely complex. Reducing it to an essence filming the pan, it requires hulking globs of energy and will and patience—things that are all depleted with age; hence the power and regression towards our pasts, and sometimes, our tendency to be stingy towards the future. Preservation: Innovation. Monuments: Babies.

My ultimate home is loving myself. As an Asian man, self-love is so hard to say, because any word(s), thoughts, ideas that even suggest self-worth, self-positivity, self-expression, are linked with conceit, not just to be eradicated, but critically, replaced with more important ideas like law or med school,

THE DIAGRAM OF DUALISTIC THINKING; HOW WE POLARIZE OURSELVES AND OTHERS

Directions: cut out words and place them anywhere you feel like on the Venn DoDT, add additional words, throw others in the trash, burn the diagram out of outrage and/or frustration.

THINGS
siblings
integrity
sexuality
materiality
wealth
looks
privilege/s
taste
envy
sex
leases
contracts
deadlines
relationships
hot
cold
baby
divorce
death
status
ego
pain
elation
house
germs
nutrition
hunger

satiation
security
insecurity
confidence
no confidence
cry
ouch
stop
go
yes
spend
laugh
stay
love
belonging
home
smart
dumb
mores
bigot
racist
agency
affection

CONCEPTS
emotion
jealousy
good
bad
indifferent
loss
need
hunk
slut
bitch
promiscuity
desire
want
funny
depravity
morality
values

like self-doubt (which keeps us tethered to elders), like an ideal of unattainable perfection (which keeps us tethered to approval—sought typically from the same elders). Exhausting.

Self-love. I cannot successfully articulate it, but it's close to what I want to say, what I'm thinking. It's not masturbating, it's not self-esteem, respect, any of the great self-things. It's much more, way more. My home, my real home is a singularly personal space inside of me. Wherever I am. The wallpaper and paint change (the supplier's inventory gets shabby as the years pass. Do you have anything without wrinkles? Do you have something less faded?), but it remains at its core like no other place. The essence of me. The Fortress of Solitude is a metaphor, no? When I go, I'll take it with me as it were; not so my house. I wouldn't want anyone following me anyway, Christ, get your own trip and leave me alone, this one's mine! I do love the kids, but can you imagine? Were members of the earliest Pharaoh's households really buried with him when he went? They were mostly men, so yeah, probably. Stick with me here: it's the modern equivalent of me extracting the promise from my children not to stick me in A Home. That kind of selfishness and fear is profound to me. I ain't no Pharaoh! The children have spent a good part of their life in the dwellings we've shared, but a lifetime of hoarded loot will mean nothing to the children other than the proceeds of an estate sale and the rental of an enormous dumpster and a subsequent dump fee. They too have moved many times in their short lives. Which house do they associate with home? I hope they'll let go and find that place inside—that place that includes memory but is not indentured to it.

The children, the (former) spouse, the last boyfriend (NEXT!) none of them have provided me with, given me a feeling of, profound rock-bottom home. We have, I believe, loved, but no person external to me can love me enough to give me security, belonging, home—that kind of love; if they're living their lives, if they're changing, how could they possibly? The sons have their own lives and I hope are finding the adult, independent-of-me, love they want and need. I will never ever doubt that the sons know they were loved by me, and I know as long as they are alive they won't be able to forget me, so it makes that whole needy trip easier—on them. Odds on, they'll start their own homes one day—well one of them anyway—like all good JA households, at least one kid never leaves home. But they are not my home. Friends, family—they can't insulate me from longing, pining, loss, sadness, despair, infirmity, my melancholy. That's my trip to make. There is no physical space that can include me, respond to me, love me—home is inanimate, nothing, an objective space. Being home is all inside, my internal living space: my shrine, my safe, my jockstrap drawer, where I keep what's emotionally and psychically sacred to me—The Temple to Myself.

I no longer believe in The Answer and haven't for a long time. At one point in my life I believed there was one answer to everything—that if I could but understand one concept, it would give me understanding and something like peace. Isn't that ludicrous? Ludicrous! It embarrasses me. Desperation and all the supporting attendant driving delusions can't make impossible things happen—can not—and there are things that are impossible (let's explore that one some more!). Yes, I don't know what I want. Yes, I don't know what love or family or home means. It's too hard to think about so I don't. With age, I sometimes feel pressure, from other people, to get this all figured out, but why? Why? WHY? When it comes up, I get better all the time at asking why—reminding myself that's their journey to make. I won't ever be rich (or poor for that matter). I'll likely not be married or well-traveled. I won't be wise, smart, handsome, happy, alone (as opposed to lonely); in the scheme of all that, where and what is home and is being there all that important?

Eureka! What.

TEMPUS FUGIT

Ion Yamazaki

Title: tempus fugit
Duration: 10 mins
Media: video
Year: 2021

This piece explores four characters (the baseball coach, a friend, my grandmother, and my father) whose ideas of masculinity I experienced in junior high and high school. The masculinities they displayed were powerful, confident, and sometimes violent. As I recall these characters through this video, my memories of their masculinity come back as well.

Throwing a rubber ball against the wall reminds me of my days on the baseball team. My coach was always coercive and violent. There was no physical violence, but his words and

his attitude were enough to strike fear into the heart of my younger self.

I bought a new pair of glasses at the time I created this piece, and the shape of the glasses looked exactly like the pair I used to wear when I was in junior high school. Back then, my school friends were concerned with how to be popular and get girlfriends. The formation and development of masculine identity among friends seemed to take place every day. To them, people with glasses were deemed unattractive and my black-rimmed pair was certainly not up to their standards of what cool boys should look like. They repeatedly told me that I should get a new frame or contact lenses, and that my glasses were one of the reasons why I did not have a girlfriend.

Of course, men are not the only inheritors of masculinity. Whenever I eat oranges, I remember my grandmother's

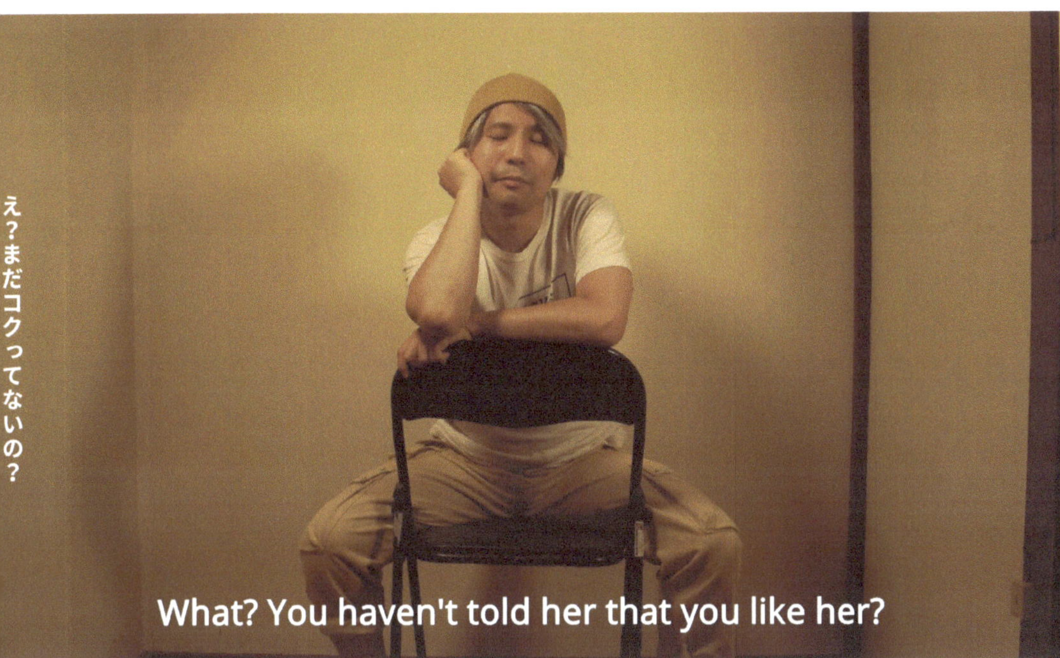

dining table where tangerines were always placed. My grandmother was a kind and caring person who embodied traditional femininity, but she also had her own strong beliefs about masculinity. She always wanted to make sure that I would become a "man" and made me listen to her words, which usually started off like, "If you are a man, you have to..."

I don't wear tank tops very often, but when I tried one for the first time in a while, I found that I looked exactly like my father. My father spent his life trying to escape the bondage of my grandfather. Yet, while he was also a victim of traditional masculinity and patriarchy, he tried to use the same oppressive system to control me. Perhaps he was escaping the spell of manhood that he himself could not control by drinking excessively every night.

Although I have been unlearning those toxic traits of

masculinity over time, these characters live on as ghosts in my memory, and will keep haunting me while telling me about their images of masculinity just as they did back then. In a sense, they are always looking at me as I am also looking back at them. The pendulum of the clock has been moving at a constant speed from that time until now, but is it only me who feels that its sound is getting louder?

A video of tempus fugit *can be viewed at* https://youtu.be/PPi5LIb2d2E *or via the QR code to the left.*

LIVING YOUR TRUE SELF

Patty Kunitsugu

I am a *Nikkei* LGBTQ+ woman living in Seattle, where I was born and raised. My life's journey—parts of which were extremely difficult and painful—has made me committed to live authentically and embrace who I am.

For many *Nikkei*, coming out is a difficult decision because the culture and traditions of the *Nikkei* community emphasize duty and devotion to family and community. These values, which I believed in and lived by, did not include LGBTQ+ people and oftentimes judged and stigmatized those with queer identities.

My grandparents immigrated to the United States in the late 1930s from Japan. In 1942, my parents and their families were interned in concentration camps during WWII. I was born ten years later in 1952, and grew up hearing their stories of the injustices, racism, and hatred that targeted the Japanese community. Having lived through those terrible experiences, I thought the *Nikkei* community would be against any form of discrimination and bias. However, that is not true. At that time, being LGBTQ+ was illegal and classified as a mental illness that carried great shame.

The Japanese community's silence around queer rights confirmed the presence of homophobia. They felt great pressure to conform to mainstream values, especially after their internment, and those values did not include supporting LGBTQ+ rights. For example, the Japanese American Citizens League (JACL) began in 1929. It wasn't until 1994 that the JACL finally took their very first action to support LGBTQ+ legislation for same-sex marriage. At the time, I was already 42 and had been with my spouse for 17 years.

Growing up, I had no one to turn to in the communities I lived in. I had to keep my identity hidden and secret. I found that it was excruciatingly painful not being able to share my feelings. Torn in many intersectional directions (woman, *Nikkei*, LGBTQ+), I became self-destructive and turned to drugs to deaden the emotions I was feeling. I hit rock bottom at 21 years old.

Sometimes, a guardian emerges to provide support and direction to those who are marginalized, rejected, and considered an outcast. I was fortunate to have found a Filipina drug counselor who helped me tremendously. She understood that Asian communities were very conservative and did not support LGBTQ+ people. She convinced me to go into several drug-rehab centers—the last one, named

Stonewall, was a place for what was then termed "sexual minorities." I got off drugs and began my new life.

Being able to finally embrace myself as queer was liberating and exhilarating! Coming out truly saved my life. I finally knew who I was and accepted it. In 1973, I came out to my parents, who, despite being *Nisei*, were amazingly supportive. They assured me that they still loved me. My father told me that he understood why I had turned to drugs because it was such a hard road to take. He felt sorry for what I had gone through. Their support, along with that of my siblings, was critical in helping me change my life. My parents had shown me a good life and always stood by my side no matter what—even if they could not fully understand what it was like being LGBTQ+.

People in the *Nikkei* community slowly found out I was queer, but never talked to my parents or me about it. It was an unspoken secret. When I came out to my friends, many whom I had grown up with could not accept it and became uncomfortable with me. I told them I was the same person, and my sexual identity should not affect our friendships.

This hurt me very deeply and makes me still wary of the community. I wanted so much to have faith in them. I wanted them to have my back. I still wanted to be a part of the community. Instead, I avoided community events and gatherings for many years.

The experiences of not being accepted or supported strengthened my resolve to fight for LGBTQ+ rights and support organizations that provide resources/support to others. At an early age, I became a human-rights advocate and activist. For example, in high school, a friend and I started the Asian Student Union in 1969. I was also active in the Civil Rights movement. Later in the 1980s, I started a Lesbians of Color group. At work, I was a Co-Lead and participant for Race and Social Justice groups.

In my continual search to find more resources and groups, I found Okaeri. I was so surprised and excited to find a group that focused on *Nikkei* LGBTQ+ people! I believe it's absolutely critical to have this kind of space. It was overwhelming and painful not to have a positive group like this when I was growing up. There is no need for anyone to feel alone. Knowing that there are others who share similar experiences and understand our culture is essential when exploring one's identity. Support, compassion, and understanding can save someone's life. Reaching out to others is what I call an act of *life support*.

It has been a difficult 70-year journey. If I had supportive resources, I could have avoided many of the painful experiences I had endured. I am still alive, transforming, and moving forward. I have been married for 45 years to a wonderful Jewish woman. Allies are vital to all human-rights movements. I'm a survivor, and I hope you, too, will find a way to live your life expressing and living your true self.

オカエリ短歌集

Hatsu Keith

多様性
溢れんばかり
ＯＫＡＥＲＩや
賛否両論
日系社会

**

社会やら
求める「らしさ」
無理せずに
土足歓迎
オカエリなさい

念願の
カミングアウト
戸惑いも
季節問わずの
我、衣替え

**

虹色祭り
世からしたら
初夏行事
おいらにしたら
日々しプライド

**

日本舞踊
幼少期から
ゲイ達者
我、願わくば
ロスの踊り子

**

オカエリの
心地良さゆえ
鳴かず飛ばずが
見て見ぬ振りの
親子関係

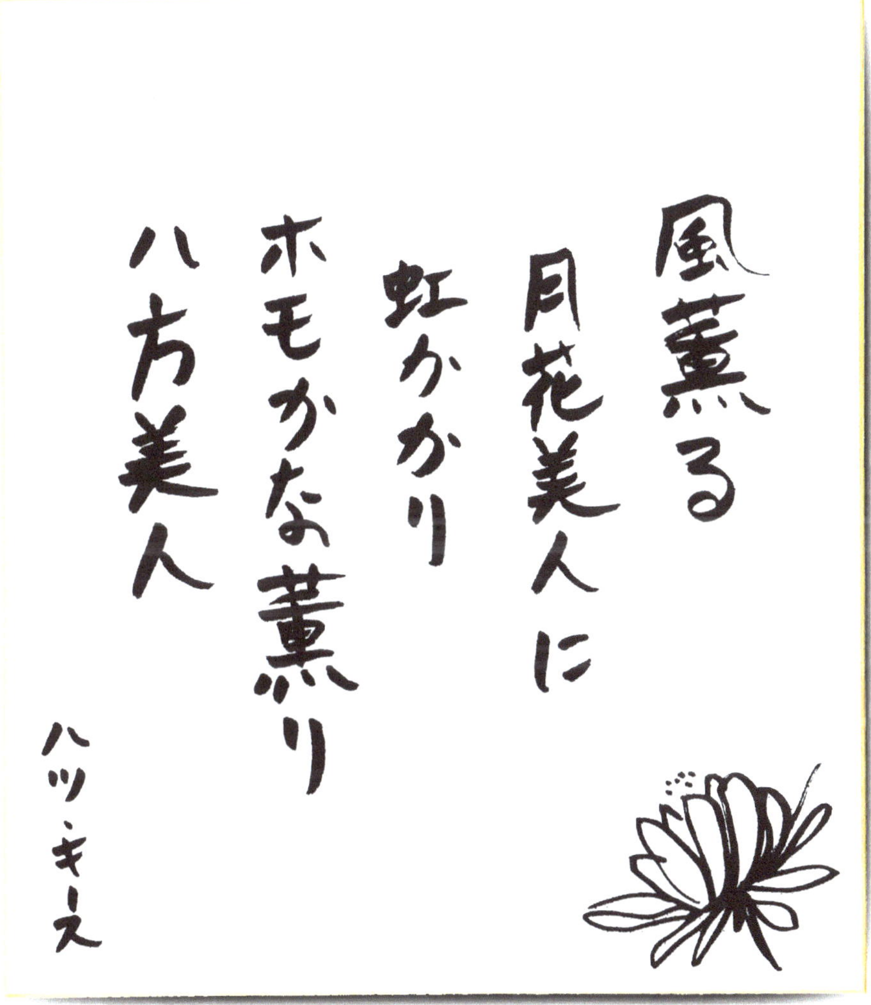

風薫る
月花美人に
虹かかり
ホモかな薫り
八方美人
ハッ・キーズ

GOING HOME
Tsukuru Fors

For 32 years since I immigrated to the U.S., traveling to Japan for me has always been "going (*iku*)" to Japan.

Never "returning (*kaeru*)." Because my life has been here. I belong here. Japan, to me, represented everything that I tried to get away from.

The irony was that I worked for a consulting firm that specifically catered to Japanese corporations operating in Japan. The job took me to Japan three times a year for 21 years, which created an interestingly emotionally awkward situation for me.

When I told my friends and acquaintances here in the States about my job, almost all of them said something like, "Wow, that must be great! You go visit family when you are there on business?"

To that, I would just shake my head from side to side and smile. "Too busy?," they would speculate, offering me an answer which I could give a nod to in response. Or, I would volunteer by saying that my family lives too far away from Tokyo for me to visit. Both of the answers were not entirely lies. They were half-truths, demonstrating my reluctance to "get into it" with them.

To tell you the truth, I've never had much of a relationship with my birth family ever since I left Japan in 1990. I lost touch with them completely when my own sister severed ties with me and forbade me to ever contact any members of the family almost ten years ago.

My relationship with my birth family symbolized my relationship with Japan. I always felt that Japan was my birth mother who never loved me back, whereas the United States was my adopted mother who embraced me, albeit with lots of issues of her own.

My relationship with Japan was a story of unrequited love. Of repeated rejections. My feelings for my motherland were tinged with fear. YES. I was afraid of Japanese society both in concept and in practicality. And I was afraid of the Japanese people.

When you have been hurt by a certain someone or a certain group of people so many times and you don't see any chance of getting them to like you, you choose to distance yourself from them as a coping strategy. I made so much effort to do just that. For those 21 years of working for the consulting firm and interacting with Japanese clients who were mostly men in management and leadership positions in small-to-medium sized companies, my hair was dyed in revolving colors: red, green, blue, silver, pink, purple, blonde, aquamarine, and emerald green. You name the color, and I can confidently say that my hair has been that color.

It was my way of signaling to the Japanese society and people that I was different. When you've already separated yourself from the pack, you no longer run the risk of being alienated from them. You've already numbed the blow.

And it produced the intended effect. My clients were willing to overlook my transgressions. They would chuckle and say, "Oh you are so American!" In their eyes, I had been so assimilated into the American way that I was no longer "really Japanese." Therefore, I could no longer be held to the Japanese standards of social protocols and propriety. It worked for me. "Yes, I am afraid I am," I would respond and put on a facial expression that was permanently stuck somewhere between a grimace and sheepish obedience. When you've already chosen to opt out, not belonging is not alienation and can't hurt you.

***

After Covid hit, everything got shut down. Companies, especially small-to-medium businesses, went into a serious money saving mode, and non-essential consultants like ours were the first thing that they let go. We lost all our clients and didn't see any ways to continue, so we disbanded. Just like that, my career of 21 years evaporated.

I had reached the end of the line, though. About one year prior, I was in a meeting with my boss and a colleague, where we strategized and prepared ourselves for an advisory meeting with a client. When we interacted with clients, no one was allowed to speak but my boss; however, we were free to contribute our opinions in a pre-meeting. I was presenting my analysis and making my case, when suddenly my boss burst out laughing. I must have given him a puzzled look, because he stopped laughing immediately. He turned to face me and said, "If you had been born a man, you would have made a good consultant."

I don't remember anything about what happened after that. Everything froze from that moment on. I must have survived the meeting somehow. I must have worked till 8 or 9pm like I had always done for the past 20 years. I don't remember how, because I was on auto-pilot for the remainder of the day. The feeling part of me checked out. I would have been broken if I had allowed myself to feel. That day my dream shattered. I had always thought if I worked hard enough, I would be rewarded. If I devoted myself enough, one day I would officially be christened with the title of "consultant." However, no such accommodation was going to be made for me. My boss had no intention of promoting me to a consultant position; I was to remain his "assistant" forever. I felt foolish and angry. I was furious with myself because I had been naive enough to think that somehow I would be an exception to the rule. How could I have believed that I was so "special"? I wanted to cut myself open so the whole world could see how much I was hurting.

On January 31st, 2021, when my last day of work came, I was already done. Spent. Hollow. Nothing more to give. The following day, February 1st, was Monday. I stepped outside in the morning, though I knew I had nowhere to go. I looked up at the blue, cloudless sky of West Los Angeles and felt an odd sense of relief. At age 50, I was a blank canvas.

***

By a strange twist of fate, what seemed like a dead-end led to the beginning of a new life. At age 50, I did the unthinkable. I came out as trans and started the process of a medical transition. Namely, I began taking testosterone. It became my weekly routine to visit a nurse clinic at a nearby Kaiser hospital.

Prior to losing my job, I had been living my life as a non-binary person for about five years. Pretty much everywhere except my work, I went by my gender-neutral adopted name, Tsukuru. At work, however, I was still known by my heavily gendered birth name and treated as a female researcher. I would never have dared to "come out" at work. I was out as lesbian and had to tolerate being ridiculed. As trans, I feared much worse. My boss would not have understood it and could have made my life so difficult that I would have been forced to quit my job.

With my job gone, I had nothing more to lose. I dived into things that I was afraid to do before. I led marches. I worked on a congressional campaign as a staffer for a remarkable young activist my child's age. I had a brief stint as a talk show host for a weekly livestream featuring other trans and non-binary people. There was no holding back. When you are jumping off a cliff, there is no "getting your feet wet." I jumped off headfirst.

Only one thing. There was one thing that I was afraid to do. Reaching out to people in my past life. Especially people whom I got acquainted with through my former career. I couldn't bring myself to open up, only to be rejected.

An important element in Japanese mythology about death is the river you cross. Once you cross over to the other side, there is no turning back. For me, transitioning was a bit like that. As weeks went by, the river that separated the present me from the old me was getting wider. Some days I looked back and marveled at how far I had come. I had come so far. Too far. There was no going back. I had moved on and never regretted it, but there was a part of me still grieving.

***

About 18 months after I had started on testosterone, I found myself in Tokyo, Japan. I was there to work on a collaborative art project on trans rights with a group of feminist artists. During my stay, I tasked myself to reestablish ties with some of my former business contacts. One such contact was a book editor fairly well known and well respected in the field, who helped us publish one of the best and longest selling books on corporate culture in the last decade. I thought to seek her advice on how to go about publishing a book on the trans liberation movement currently unfolding in the U.S. I worked up all the courage that I could possibly muster and contacted her. To my surprise, she agreed to see me without a moment of hesitation.

It was a Friday evening at about 6pm. I had just left a meeting with the editor and was walking to a public square in Ikebukuro where I was to meet a friend. I was going over the session with the editor and felt grateful for the attention that she had given to my project. She was very straightforward and upfront about not being able to help me publish the book herself. However, she took the time to read the proposal, pointed out what had piqued her interest, and gave me several options to explore. I appreciated her cordiality and kindness. The December air was crisp on my skin, but there was warmth in my heart.

While navigating through the sea of people who had just come out of their offices and hurrying to meet their loved ones or friends to enjoy the start of the weekend, my thoughts wandered back to the editor. I kept thinking how different she seemed. I remembered her being aloof and unapproachable, but this time she was courteous, friendly even. I knew that she had become a mother a few years ago. Maybe motherhood changed her.

I was strolling inside the corridors of Ikebukuro station, not in too much of a hurry since I had plenty of time. I was remembering how the district of Ikebukuro scared me when I was there on business years ago. It felt simply too chaotic. Too many people. Too much noise. This time around, too, it was chaotic. There were so many people passing by that I had to choose my path carefully and change directions accordingly. It felt a bit like an old-fashioned video game where you had to dodge bullets or avoid crashing into oncoming traffic. There was still so much noise, but I was enjoying myself, taking all of it in.

Then, something clicked in me. I was hit by a realization. Or a better way to put it would be that a possible consideration was whispered into my consciousness by the voice of the universe. "What if it wasn't the editor that had changed? What if it was me?"

What if I had changed? It hit me so hard that I had to stop in the middle of the track to catch my breath. I heard a man behind me groan in mild annoyance; I stopped so abruptly that he almost bumped into me. I had to take my phone out of my pocket and pretend to check messages. When I looked up once again to face the crowd of random strangers, everything made sense. All the puzzle pieces had fallen into their place.

Yes, I had changed. Standing there in the middle of the Ikebukuro station, I was as raw and real as ever before. I had gone back to my original state without all the gender bullshit. No one was telling me anymore what I should wear or how I should behave. No one was policing me and telling me that I should smile more or use a softer tone of voice. I was unapologetic, 100% unadulterated me. For the first time in my life, there I stood as "me" in the streets of Tokyo, Japan, the country where I was born 51 years ago.

And I was seeing the scenery, and the people, with my own eyes for the first time.

You may think I am being overly dramatic. It might have been that the Xmas illuminations were playing tricks on me, but I swear on my life that every moment that my eyes captured during the two-week trip to Japan, the first one since I had begun my transition, seemed so vivid and real. It was not the Japan that I remembered: Dull. Exhausted. Rigid. Protocoled. Fake. Even mean. I realized that that was how I had felt about my own existence, and in looking out at the world, I had been looking at my own reflections.

On the streets of Tokyo, Japan, on that night in December 2022, I was remembering and reliving the past 21 years of my life when I had spent at least three times a year in Japan on business, two weeks at a time. Often when I was having dinner with clients, I would have a sort of out-of-body experience, where I was observing me entertaining the clients. And I would think to myself, "who is that woman?" She had a smile plastered onto her face and was laughing about something that she did not even think was remotely funny. And I, the person who was outside of her body looking at her, would feel so disgusted and numb, because everything was so fake.

All my life up until I began my transition, I felt so fake to myself, and people to me seemed like cardboard figures. There was always an invisible sheet of plexiglass between me and them. They couldn't relate to me, and neither could I to them.

In that hallway in Ikebukuro station, I felt that I could reach out and touch them for the first time in my life. Feel their warmth. I saw the Japanese people as individuals for the first time. They were, just like me, packed with pain, sorrow, anger, frustrations, and contradictions of their own, and yet they still carried on, for they also had joy, pride, and love inside them, just like I did.

Tears were running down my cheeks, and I was glad that a mask covered half of my face and made it less obvious. I was grateful that I had gotten to see Japan, the country where I was born, and its people, with my own eyes for the first time. I don't know if Japan, my motherland, welcomed me with open arms, but at least she saw the real me and acknowledged my existence. That, to me, meant that finally I was going home.

帰路につく
Tsukuru Fors

　32年前にアメリカに移住して以来、ぼくにとって日本への旅はいつも「日本に行く」だった。

　けっして「帰る」ではない。ぼくの生活はいつもここ（アメリカ）にあったから。ぼくにとっての日本は、ぼくが逃げようとしたすべてのものを意味した。

　皮肉なことに、ぼくは21年間、日本企業を専門にサービスを提供するコンサルティング会社に働いていた。その関係で年に三回は日本に行く機会があった。これは、ぼくを感情的に微妙な場所におとしいれた。

　友だちや知人に仕事の話をすると、きまってこんな言葉がかえってきた。「それはいいね！出張のついでに家族に会いにいったりするの？」

　それに対しては、ぼくはいつも首を横に振ってただにっこりするのだった。「忙しくてそんなヒマはないか？」たいていの場合、向こうからぼくが肯定のしるしにうなづきやすい返事を用意してくれた。そうでないときは、ぼくのほうから家族は東京から遠く離れたところに住んでいて簡単に訪ねていける距離でないことを説明した。「忙しい」も「遠すぎる」もまったくの嘘ではなかった。いうなれば「ほとんどほんとう」のことだ。深く入り込んで言い訳する手間を省くための。

　正直にいうと、1990年に日本をあとにしてから、ぼくはぼくの血のつながった家族とほとんど関係をもってこなかった。10年ほど前に姉がぼくとの絶縁を宣言し、二度と家族の誰とも連絡をとってくれるなと言い渡されてからは、まったく音信が途絶えてしまった。

　ぼくと家族との関係は、ぼくと日本との関係に象徴的に類似する。ぼくにとって日本は、ぼくをけっして愛してくれなかった産みの母親だった。一方で、アメリカは、ぼくを受け容れてくれた養母だ。彼女は彼女で、いろんな問題を抱えているにせよ。

　ぼくと日本との関係は、報われない愛のものがたりだ。度重なる拒絶の歴史だ。母なる国へのぼくの想いは恐怖に染まっている。そう。ぼくは日本社会にずっと恐怖を抱いてきた。概念的にも実践においても。そしてずっと「日本人」という人たちが怖かった。

　ある人やある人たちから幾度も傷つけられて、そしてその人たちが自分を「好き」になるように仕向ける望みがほとんどないと悟ったとき、人は自分から距離をとることを選ぶものだ。それが生き残るための手だてだからだ。ぼくもあらゆる努力をしてそれを試みた。コンサルティング会社に働いて中小企業のお偉いさん（ほとんどが男性だった）と関わっていたころは、髪を常に色とりどりに染めていた。赤、緑、青、シルバー、ピンク、パープル、ブロンド、アクアマリン、エメラルド・グリーン・・・。思いつく色を言ってもらったら、十中八九その色に染めたことがあると、自信をもって言える。

　それは日本社会に対して、ぼくは「ちがう」ということを知らしめるぼくなりの策略だった。自ら群れを離れてしまえば、疎外されるリスクを負うことはもうない。もうそれほど痛みを感じることもないのだ。

　そしてそれは思い通りの効果をもたらした。およそ日本人らしくないぼくのふるまいを、クライアントたちは往々にして咎めようとはしなかった。声を出さずに笑って、「〇〇さんはまったくアメリカ人だなあ！」と言うだけだった。彼らの目には、ぼくはとてもアメリカナイズされて映ったので、もはや

「ほんとうの」日本人ではなかったのだ。だから、ぼくのふるまいが日本的な決まりや礼儀作法の基準に従って裁かれることはなかった。それはぼくにとっては好都合だった。「ええ、そうですね」ぼくは答えて、しかめ面と控えめなへつらいの中間点で永遠に固まってしまったような表情をはりつけた。自分から「いち抜けた」と宣言してしまえば、属さないことは疎外ではなく、それに傷つけられることはない。

＊＊＊

コロナウイルスの感染抑止のために、何もかもがシャットダウンした。中小企業はとくに節約モードに入り、ぼくたちみたいな「べつになくても困らないコンサルタント契約」はまっさきにカットされた。ぼくの勤めていた会社はすべてのクライアントをなくし、それ以上続けていくすべが見つからなかったので、解散した。そんなふうに実にあっけなく、21年間かけて築いたぼくのキャリアは、一夜にして消えてなくなった。

　そのころ、正直言ってもうすでに終点に行きついたと感じてた。その一年くらい前に、ちょっと立ち直れないような、深い傷をつくる出来事があったからだ。ある日、ぼくは上司と同僚と三人で、クライアントとのコンサル・セッションに向けて戦略を練る準備ミーティングに参加していた。クライアントと接するときには、上司だけが話すことが許されていたが、準備ミーティングの際にはぼくたちも意見を述べることができた。ぼくが自分の分析をプレゼンして、クライアントにはこうアドバイスすべきと熱弁をふるっていた最中に、とつぜん上司が声をあげて笑い出した。ぼくが怪訝な顔をしたんだろう。彼はすぐに笑うのをやめて、ぼくの方を見て、こう言った。「きみが男に生まれていたら、いいコンサルタントになっただろうな」

　そのあとのことは何も覚えていない。そこからすべてが凍りついた。おそらく、ミーティングはやりすごしたにちがいない。ぼくが20年間毎日のようにそうしてきたように、夜の八時、九時くらいまで働いたにちがいない。でも覚えていない。ミーティングでのあの瞬間から、自動操縦モードだったからだ。ぼくの感情中枢はストライキを宣言した。もしあの痛みを感じていたら壊れてしまっただろうから。あの日、ぼくの夢はこなごなに砕けた。がんばって働けば、報われるとずっと思っていた。仕事に身を捧げることで、いつか「コンサルタント」の肩書が与えられると思っていたのだ。でも、そんな特別なはからいがあるはずがなかった。上司は、ぼくをコンサルタントに昇格させる気なんかサラサラなかったのだ。ぼくは永久に彼の「アシスタント」にとどまる運命だったのだ。ぼくは自分の愚かさに怒りを感じた。自分は例外だなんて、なんで信じたのだろう。自分は「特別」だなんて思えた自分はなんて世間知らずな馬鹿者だっただろう。自分をまっぷたつに切り裂いて見せたら、どれだけ傷ついているかがみんなにわかるだろうか、そんな狂ったことを考えていた。

　2021年1月31日、会社出勤の最後の日が訪れたとき、ぼくの中ではもうすべてが終わっていた。もう与えるものは何もなかった。翌日、2月1日は月曜日だった。行くところなんてないことはわかっていたけれど、その朝、ぼくは家の外に出て、空を見上げた。ウェストロサンゼルスの雲一つない空を眺めて、なんだか奇妙な安堵を感じた。50歳にして、ぼくは空っぽのキャンバスだった。

＊＊＊

　奇妙な運命のいたずらで、行き止まりだと思ったのが新しい人生のはじまりになった。50歳にして、ぼくは「ありえない」ことをした。トランスとしてカミングアウトして、性別移行のプロセスをはじめた。もっと具体的にいえば、テストステロン治療をはじめた。近所のカイザーの病院を訪ね、看護師さんに注射を打ってもらうことがぼくの毎週のスケジュールに加わった。

　仕事をなくす前の五年間ほど、ぼくはノンバイナリーとして生きていた。仕事場を除いてはほとんどすべての場所で、男、女のどちらともとれる中性的な名前、「つくる」で通っていた。でも仕事場では、生まれたときに授かった女性名で呼ばれ、「女性の」リサーチャーとして扱われていた。仕事場でカミングアウトしようなんて、考えたこともなかった。レズビアンとしてカミングアウトしていたけれど、それでもジョークのネタにされることがしょっちゅうだった。トランスだなんてことが知れたら、もっとひどい扱いを受けただろう。上司の理解を得るなんてありえなかったし、居心地が悪くなって、会社をやめるのを強いられることは目に見えていた。

　でも仕事がなくなってしまったから、これ以上失うものはもう何も
なかった。それまで恐れてできなかったことに飛び込んだ。マーチを企画した。
国会議員候補の選挙キャンペーンをスタッフとして手伝った。その候補は
自分の子供くらい若い、驚くほど聡明で勇気のあるアクティビストで、それ以来
彼はぼくの無二の友人になった。トランスやノンバイナリーの仲間たちを
毎週ゲストに呼ぶトークショーのホストをほんの少しの間だったけど務めた。
ぼくを引き止めるものはもう何もなかった。崖から飛び降りるときに、「まず
足を濡らして」なんてことはない。頭からいちどに飛び込むだけだ。

　でも一つだけ、ただ一つ怖くてできないことがあった。移行前のぼくを
知る人たちに連絡をとることだった。とくに前職をとおして知り合った
人たちだ。思い切って心を開いて、そして拒絶されたらどんなに痛いだろう。。。
そう考えると、どうしても一歩を踏み出すことができなかった。

　「死」に関して日本人なら誰でも知っているといっても間違いないことに、
「三途の川」がある。いちど向こう岸に渡ったらもう戻ることはない。ぼくに
とって性別移行はそれに似ていた。時が経つにつれて、現在のぼくと昔のぼくを
隔てる川はどんどん大きくなっていった。ときに後ろを振り返って、なんて
遠くに来たんだろうと驚くことがあった。ほんとうに遠くまで来てしまった。
もう戻ることはない。昔の自分をあとにしたことに、後悔はなかった。でも
どこかに、失ったものを悼む自分はいた。

＊＊＊

　テストステロンをはじめてからおよそ18か月後くらいに、ぼくは東京
にいた。フェミニスト・アーティストのグループとトランスの権利に関する
コラボ・プロジェクトをやるために日本に来たのだ。滞在中に、前職で
知り合った数人の人たちに連絡をとり、「つくる」として改めて付き合いを
はじめた。そのうちひとりは出版業界でかなり名の知れた編集者で、
前職でぼくの上司が出版をした際にお世話をしてくれた人だった。

彼女の手掛けた僕たちの本は、過去10年間のうちに日本語で書かれた企業文化の本の中では、最もよく読まれたベストセラー、ロングセラーのひとつとなった。ぼくはアメリカで現在進行中のトランス解放運動についての本を書きたいと思い、その出版についてその人の意見をききたいと思ったのだ。ありったけの勇気を振り絞って彼女にコンタクトをしたら、驚いたことに、ふたつ返事で会うことを承諾してくれた。

　それは金曜日の六時ごろだった。編集者とのミーティングを終えて、池袋の広場で友人と会うために足を進めていた。頭の中で編集者との会話を反芻して、ぼくのプロジェクトへのその人の真摯な対応に深い感謝を覚えていた。彼女自身は出版を手伝えないことに関してはじめから率直に正直に述べたうえで、その人は丁寧に企画書を読み、彼女自身がどこに興味を惹かれたか、そして、出版を実現するのにどんなアプローチが考えられるか、プロとしてその人なりの意見を聞かせてくれた。その人の真心と親切な態度に心を打たれた。師走の空気は肌に冷たかったけれども、ぼくの心はほっこり温かかった。

　それぞれの職場をあとにし、週末のはじまりを家族や友人と楽しもうと目的地に向けて急ぐ人たちの波を潜り抜けながら、ぼくの思考はふたたびしぜんとたった今会ってきたばかりの編集者に戻るのだった。彼女がとても変わったなあと感じていた。前職で付き合いのあったころには、ちょっと浮世離れしていて近づきがたい人だと思っていたけれど、今日会ったその人は思いやりに溢れていた。フレンドリーでさえあった。数年前にお子さんが生まれたと聞いていたけれど、もしかしたら、その影響かもしれなかった。

　そんなことを考えながらぼくは池袋駅の構内を歩いていた。待ち合わせの時刻まではまだ余裕があったから、急ぐわけでもなく。何年も前に出張で訪れた際に、池袋の街が怖かったことを思い出していた。単純に煩雑すぎるように感じて。人が多すぎて。そしてうるさすぎて。そして今も、混沌としていることに変わりはなかった。たくさんの人が後からあとから溢れてきては行き交う中で、気を配って歩みを選び、人にぶつからないようにときどき方向を変えなくてはならなかった。それは弾丸を避けたり、猛スピードで向かってくる対向車の間をすり抜ける昔ながらのビデオゲームを思わせた。池袋の街は相変わらず喧噪としていたけれども、ぼくはそれを楽しんでいた。すべてをのみこんで、味わっていた。

その瞬間にはっとした。「ああ、そうか」と思った。言い方を変えれば、世界をつかさどる何かの声が、ぼくの意識に向けてこうささやいた。「変わったのは編集者ではなく、きみだったとしたなら？」

変わったのは他の誰でもなく、ぼくだったとしたなら？その考えに打たれて、ぼくは道の真ん中で立ち止まってしまった。そして呼吸をととのえた。後ろを歩いていた男の人がちょっと不満そうにうなる声が聞こえた。ぼくがあまりに急に立ち止まったので、ぶつかりそうになったのだ。ぼくはポケットからスマホを取り出して、メッセージをチェックするふりをした。次にスマホから顔をあげると、見知らぬ人の群れがふたたび目に入ってきて、そのとき、すべてが明らかになった。パズルのピースがしかるべきところに収まったように。

そうだ。ぼくは変わった。ぼくはそれ以上ないくらいまっさらで、リアルな状態で、池袋駅の真ん中に立っていた。性別というしち面倒くさいものをとっぱらった原点に戻って。もう誰も、ぼくにどのように装い、どのように振るまえと命令したりしない。ぼくの一挙一動を取り締まり、もっと微笑むべきだとか、やさしいトーンで話せとか、うるさく言う人はいない。ぼくはもうぼくがぼくであることに、言い訳したり、あやまったりなんかしない。ここに立っているのは、100パーセントごまかしのない、ありのままのぼくだ。51年前にぼくが生まれた日本という国の、東京の街頭に、生まれてはじめて、ぼくは「ぼく」として立っていた。

そして生まれてはじめて、ぼく自身の目をとおして、日本の景色を、そしてそこに住む人たちを眺めていた。

人はおおげさだとぼくを笑うかもしれない。キラキラしたクリスマスのイルミネーションに惑わされたのかもしれない。でもこれだけは誓って言える。性別移行以来はじめての日本滞在のあの二週間で目にしたすべての瞬間はとても鮮明でリアルだった。それはぼくが以前に知っていた日本ではなかった。

色あせていて、疲弊していて、堅苦しくて、がんじがらめで、にせもので、いじわるでさえある。以前、ぼくが見ていた日本の印象は、ぼくが自分自身の存在と、世界に対して抱いていた感情と同じだった。ぼくは鏡に映る自分の姿を見ていたのだった。

　2022年12月の夜、東京の街頭で、ぼくは過去21年間、仕事で日本を訪れていたときのことを思い出して、追体験していた。クライアントとの会食の席で、幽体離脱のような体験をすることがあった。クライアントと談笑している自分を、すこし離れたところで自分が観察している。傍観者である自分は、登場人物である自分を眺めて、「あの女は誰だ？」と思う。紋切り型の微笑みを顔に貼り付けて、ちっとも面白いと思わない何かについて笑っている彼女がいる。彼女を見ている自分は身のもだえるほどの嫌悪感を感じると同時に、何も感じない自分を呪っている。すべては救いなくにせものだ。

　性別移行をはじめるまで、ずっと、自分自身がにせものだと感じてた。そして周りのすべての人が段ボールの切り抜きのように思えた。自分と「ひと」とは常に目に見えないプレキシガラスで隔たれていた。彼らはぼくとつながることはできなかったし、ぼくも彼らとつながることはできなかった。

　池袋駅の構内で、あのとき、生まれてはじめて、ぼくは手を伸ばせば、彼らに触れられると感じた。ひとのぬくもりを感じた。はじめて、日本の人たちを、集団としてではなく、「人ひとり」として感じられた。ぼくと同じように、痛みや、悲しみや、怒りや、苛立ちや、それぞれの矛盾をいっぱいに抱えたひととして。それでいて、彼らはみんな、生きようとしていた。ぼくと同じように、みんな、よろこびを、自負を、そして愛を、内に秘めているから。

　涙がほほを伝って流れ落ちていた。マスクで顔の半分は隠れていたから、泣き顔がそれほどあからさまでないことがありがたかった。日本を、自分が生まれた国を、そしてその国に住む人たちを、はじめて自分の目を通して見られたことがありがたかった。自分の「母国」である日本が、両腕を広げてぼくを抱きしめてくれたかどうかはわからない。でも、少なくとも、ありのままの「ぼく」を、ぼくの存在を見てくれた。それは、ぼくにとっては、「おかえり」だった。

04
"YOUR HOME WILL ALWAYS BE

MY GAYNESS WAS MORE POWERFUL THAN ANY PRAYER THAT COULD BE IMPOSED
SELF-PORTRAITS
WAITING HERE FOR YOU, ALWAYS

ON FAIRIES AND DUST

Mariko Rooks

i.
The kind of fairytale I've always wanted to read begins with
the tap of a soft makeup brush against the sink,
a story that echoes between us as she brings the glittering
highlighter to my face,
eyes far closer to each other than I'd ever hoped they'd be.
her wrist arcs upward and suddenly
gold is shimmering against my skin
dust sweeping across high cheekbones and
caressing the bows between our lips
glowing across the bathroom floor,
inhaling
all the words we cannot say.

ii.

smearing gold across the contours of my skin

is fun when everything is make pretend

but if our history tells us anything

it's that far too often we're cast in stories that are real

but never true.

It only takes one girl to make me believe in magic and

it only takes being called a girl once for me to stop believing in

my own existence.

The dust across my cheeks writhes into a vice choking my neck,

golden like

horse stalls and deserts like[1]

babies choking on grains of sand spit between barrack struts like

birth control pills across the tiles of a gray dorm bathroom like

spitting up any kind of prescription against the mirror of any

"girls" bathroom like

don't make waves.

Over time, this kind of dust congeals until you forget that you

cannot breathe[2]

coating the corners of our attics and

smearing clumps of thick residue over our history

until we replace *yoshiya*[3] with *yoshinoya*

forget men in kimono and tender embraces and

two farmers pressing white cotton shirts together

against a polaroid frame.

---

1 Homage to Janice Mirikitani's "Breaking Silence."

2 Tony McDade. Layleen Xtravaganza Cubilette-Polanco. All of the QTBIPOC killed by police each day.

3 Nobuko Yoshiya was a Japanese lesbian literature pioneer in the 1920s.

iii.

Often, I think about the dust that coated my grandmother's home.
Even when she became too weak to run a gentle feather
duster and cutting eyes
over innumerable nooks and crannies,
she still powdered dust across her face each morning,
redrew eyes and lips over a childhood where she looked like me.
I think about her dark nine-year-old skin framed by tomboy short hair
our sharp knees poking through shorts pulled up to her waist
Django Jane screaming through Japanese rice paddies.[4]
I wish I could tell her the words for what we were,
or at least what I hoped she could have been.

Confession #1: When I am angriest with my grandmother,
even all these years later, I imagine her queer as compensation
for all the time that curdled in between us.
At my queerest, I remember there is so much more power in
the soft ambiguity of the never-known.

iv.

Confession #2: I want to tear down the world at its seams
hair long like charging on the backs of horses against colonizers
(any colonizers)
until I devour it whole,

pretty like the pale honeyed boy standing on the edge of a sunset,[5]

---

4 "Runnin' outta space in my damn bandwagon
Remember when they used to say I look too mannish
Black girl magic, y'all can't stand it
Y'all can't ban it, made out like a bandit
They been tryin' hard just to make us all vanish"
- Janelle Monae, "Django Jane,"
5 https://www.instagram.com/p/CniXyEdyhLF/?hl=en

I want to be ground down to my bones

instead of stripped down to my parts,

plantation-thin[6] skin peeled back until I am raw and screaming.

Cut the wires and circuits that puppeteer me into the techno-orient

peel off the madam butterfly wings

strip me bare until I am nothing left but myself

and coat us all in flowers instead.[7]

v.

I was six years old when I learned that our pillows slowly get heavier,

that the silk and cotton slowly accumulate the memory of our

faces and lips.

Dust is, simply,

the shedding of our skin.

The past and the metamorphosis.

The dust reminds us that even when we do know or believe

(in) ourselves,

we float across the air every day.

"Here," say the motes spinning in the afternoon light

we are the proof that we have always been here long enough

to accumulate,

across cheekbones and attics and butterfly wings,

particles of ourselves dancing whenever we catch the setting sun.

---

6   [TW medical, anti-Black violence] I think a lot about how many Black enslaved people,
like my ancestors, were the violent subjects of plantation experimentation in the name
of medicine. Doctors would peel enslaved skin off layer by layer in attempt to "discover"
what made Black people "Black," much as medical violence has been enacted in the name
of discovering what makes queer and trans people "divergent." I feel immense amount
of gender dysmorphia when people strip my gender presentation away to assign me
womanhood, a specific kind of violence that feels as if my skin is being ripped off or peeled
away.

7 https://www.instagram.com/p/CnByUi4J-ws/?hl=en

BECOMING SAKURA

Sakura Okubo

My legal name is Koji Tom and my preferred name is Sakura. I'm a second generation Japanese American and I am currently transitioning from male to female. I'm 53 years old, born and raised in Chicago, IL. I'm bisexual (mostly attracted to women) and have paranoid schizophrenia and PTSD. I'm partially blind in my left eye and have a left shoulder injury, a learning disability, and an intellectual disability.

My father recently passed away and I currently live with my mom, who is 83. I rely on her for everything, but she will never understand me. The way she first found out that I was buying women's clothing was because the clothes were in the living room. We fought a little bit and she told me that I could not buy or wear women's clothing ever again. She said that I would become homeless and die alone. To this day, my mom doesn't want me to wear women's clothing or makeup and she always cuts my hair. My mom is aggressive and I am living a double life.

Growing up, I had a really bad childhood. I only spoke Japanese at home, so I was bullied at school because I couldn't speak English well. I also had no brothers or sisters, and no other relatives in Chicago. I started to notice differences between boys and girls when I was in kindergarten. I always saw girls dressing up in whatever they wanted, but the boys only wore shirts and pants. I wished I could wear whatever I wanted but I always had to wear shirts and pants.

In the summer of the third grade, I drew a picture of myself naked with a doctor next to me holding my penis and testicles in the air. That was when I first started thinking that I was a girl. I would continue to draw more pictures and hide them from my mom. Years later, when my mom was cleaning my room she found the picture I drew in third grade. She didn't say anything, but she destroyed the picture and ripped it up. It made me feel embarrassed and scared.

Another time in elementary school, I had a sleepover at my friend's house and we both dressed up as girls. My friend went out in the yard and danced around. I wanted to join him, but I didn't want to get caught or seen by police if they were in the neighborhood. My friend told me that the police target people who are crossdressing or are transgender and that scared me. Even though I didn't go outside in girl's clothing, it's still a good memory for me because I was able to dress as a girl.

One other positive memory is when my mom helped me

put on lipstick. It was during the summer when I was still in elementary school, and I don't remember if I asked her to wear lipstick—it just happened. She put it on me and I remember her saying I looked cute. Hearing her say that made me feel good. This was the only time I wore makeup growing up and I'm not sure why it didn't happen again.

Despite those positive memories, there were many more negative ones. During Christmas one year, my mom and I went to a toy store to shop for some toys for my relatives in Japan. She pointed me toward the Barbie section and asked for my opinion about which doll I thought was best to play with. I picked out Barbie accessories like clothes and shoes and my mom bought them. I really wanted to play with the Barbies, but my mom sent them all to my relatives.

Manga and anime have always been a really important part of my life. Imagining myself as the characters in the anime I watched helped me to realize I was trans because I identified with female characters. My favorite anime of all time is *Card Captor Sakura*. Sakura is cute and I always wanted to dress up like her, especially in her red battle costume from the series. That is actually why I chose my name Sakura. I grew up watching this anime and I even have the DVDs. My ultimate dream right now is to own a cosplay store where a person can come in, pick a cosplay costume, get the right materials, measurements, and accessories, and have a professionally done photoshoot.

I've always dreamed of dressing up in cosplay too, and the one time I've done it was on Halloween at a movie theater I used to work at about twenty years ago. My manager said everyone could dress up however they wanted. I wanted to find a Sailor Moon costume, but all that was available was a Minnie Mouse costume. At the time, the vocabulary for being trans wasn't well-known, so I thought of myself as a crossdresser. My coworkers dared me to dress up like a woman, so my first costume was a ballerina. I showed my coworkers my costume in front of everyone at the concession stand. They were surprised. I was expecting them to say something negative, but they didn't. They were nice about it.

My next costume was dressing up as Minnie Mouse. My coworkers were really blown away by this one because I looked so good! Even my manager was surprised. I was the only person at work who crossdressed. Since I was dressed as a woman at work, I didn't know how I was going to use the restroom. I thought that people would make mean comments or even do something dangerous to me. So, I actually wore an adult diaper so I didn't have to use the restroom while I was at work. The customers complimented my outfit and I only got one negative comment from a teen girl. Dressing up as a woman felt normal and I felt relieved. It felt like this was how I was supposed to be.

Currently, I can only dress as a woman at certain times when I'm out of the house. I used to bring a woman's outfit to my doctor's appointments, change in a gender neutral restroom, go to my appointment, and then change back into men's clothes before going home. Sometimes when I meet up with my trans friends, I can wear women's clothing around them. When I come home though, I have to hide my clothes from my mother.

I thought I was the only Japanese American transgender woman. But when I found Okaeri, I realized there were lots of other transgender Japanese Americans and others across the LGBTQ+ spectrum. I really liked that they had discussion groups in English because my Japanese is not as good, so that's why I decided to join. I felt like I had someplace I belonged to, and I hope to meet my Okaeri friends in person someday.

Right now I am secretly taking hormone replacement therapy and freezing my sperm. But I cannot wear women's clothes openly or change my name. When my mom passes away though, I can get gender affirmation surgeries like facial feminization surgery, laser hair removal, breast augmentation, and bottom surgery. Thinking of my future is a mixture of sadness and hope. The sadness is from thinking about my mom passing away and me being on my own. But I'm hopeful because I'd finally be free to live as a woman, the way I was always meant to be.

(UN)BROKEN

Justen Quan

For a long time, I've struggled with reconciling my Japanese American (JA) identity and my queer identity. While the JA community that most of us grew up in can be a source of support, comfort, and growth, it can also be stifling and isolating for queer folks or those of us who are different.

Growing up, to feel accepted in the JA community often meant to dismiss, subdue, or, in most cases, blatantly hide my queerness. Especially within the JA basketball community, I always felt the need to conceal elements of my personality that were considered feminine and embody the masculinity that was expected of me. With the JA community being so tight-knit, I constantly felt judgment from others too—peers, friends, parents, even grandparents—and a suffocating fear of others questioning my sexuality.

Self-Portrait, watercolor on paper

Once I came out in my early twenties, I felt the need to almost overcorrect this by completely dismissing my JA identity and the JA community. As I began to blossom as a gay man and started unraveling how my upbringing had hindered and delayed this process, I felt a lot of anger and resentment towards the JA community. I felt like I had wasted so much time being ashamed of my queer identity—one that had taken so much courage to understand, love, and uplift—just to fit into a community that I felt did not deserve to know this part of me. There was a lot of pain there, feeling as if these two identities couldn't coexist.

Now that I'm in my late twenties and have taken the time to unpack a lot of this anger, I've realized that I shouldn't reject one part of myself just for the sake of another—the pieces of my identity are intertwined in a way that makes me who I am and shouldn't have to be experienced separately. Truthfully, I can't say that I've fully reconciled the inner turmoil between these two aspects of my identity yet. But, confronting this pain has brought me closer to understanding who I am; a journey that still feels like a work in progress but is healing nonetheless.

Okaeri, to me, means embracing all of this. It means welcoming all parts of yourself. It means leaning on your community for love and support. It means returning to yourself—giving yourself time and space to heal, learn, and accept.

This self-portrait represents the idea that community can be there to help you pick up the pieces despite being part of the reason you're broken in the first place. The adversities we face should not have to be faced alone; leaning into community, family, and friends, rather than shunning myself has helped me live more authentically and reclaim my identity as a queer Japanese American.

我慢して
(≠頑張って!)
THERE ARE TWO KINDS OF PERSEVERANCE
C.K.

Being in my early twenties has meant a tidal wave of growth and change—often more than I think I can handle, to be honest. And amidst all of this growing and changing, I get surprised whenever I return to my family home: while I've been across the country transforming into a different version of myself, this place has stayed obstinately the same. It makes home feel like an unfamiliar place sometimes, which frightens me.

I am afraid of the day that *okaeri* stops being the right greeting for me. One day, I may stay away so long that it stops counting as me "coming back home." Or I might become someone they don't feel comfortable welcoming home anymore.

My queerness is not something that I've shared with my family yet, and I'm not sure that I ever will. It's strange

我慢して。

because it's such an un-hidden part of my life everywhere else. But when I'm with my family, I am a nesting doll: outside, you see a half-hidden girl who stays closed as she houses something precious inside her. Inside, you'll find an out-and-proud bisexual Asian-American woman who is tired, admittedly, but open. Will the inside doll ever get to hear おかえりなさい from my family? Will she ever be welcomed? Welcomed home? Welcomed back? しかも, in Japanese?

UNTITLED (SELF-PORTRAIT)

Ken Takeuchi

The image had been in my mind for some time, insisting to come out for at least a few weeks, if not months. It was an image of an angel crouched down with his back against a wall, deeply troubled, with eyes closed and holding himself in dreaming. His large wings are nailed to the wall, rendering him immobile.

A few years after graduating from college, I moved into an old brownstone walkup in Brooklyn, NY. It was the halcyon days of the mid-90s, when I felt endless possibilities to follow my dreams. During the day, I was spending long hours learning to manage equipment and working on challenging projects at a sound studio. When I finally got off work, I'd walk down a block to happy hour at Splash, a popular gay bar in Chelsea, where I'd become invisible. After many nights of

Untitled (Self-portrait), 35mm print, 20"x30" (2005)
- Ken Takeuchi

self-medication, the angel couldn't wait much longer. So, I had to help get him out onto a canvas.

I got a large canvas cut and put it up on a wall, sketched the outlines with charcoal, and began to paint. All the hours of stressing at work and looking over my shoulder for fear of being caught without a work permit seemed to slowly dissolve into meditation as I put down layers of paint. With thick white strokes showing his powerful wings and gradation of primary colors of sunset projecting his dreamscape of desire above, the angel became my own reflection full of conflicting emotions: despair of never being good enough, blinding fear for the unknown future, hating myself for every failure in love, and having to hold myself because no one else would. During the weeks of painting, I felt the reflection becoming solid, like the pieces of an impossible puzzle suddenly and inextricably fitting as they were meant to be. When the painting told me it was done, I finally began to comprehend the gestalt; no matter how impossible it seems, life is worth living because love is eternal.

The painting hung in the small room of my apartment for seven years, where it saw the Twin Towers fall and experienced the Northeast blackout. After traveling through the South for a year, it came back home in a FedEx box. Now in a frame, I put the painting back on the wall where it belongs.

One late afternoon, I walked into the room bathed in lavender light. On the opposite wall from the painting, a framed round mirror reflects the angel and I catch myself under him. I grabbed my camera and took a photo of us, me carrying him on the shoulder. Like twin flames, we were meant to be whole again during our journey. When in doubt, I look at the portrait and remind myself that wherever I'm at in my path, I will always have a place to come home to.

A PRODIGAL SON'S RETURN TO THE VILLAGE:
A REFLECTION ON GROWING UP GAY IN (AND OUT) OF THE NIKKEI COMMUNITY
Eric Arimoto

In 1983, I left the *Nikkei* community to join the Army right out of high school, never to return to the "village." As a closeted gay, fourth generation Japanese American (JA) whose parents were outsiders in their own ways, I never felt rooted in the community and I could not wait to leave it. The *Nikkei* community felt so self-conscious and provincially obsessed with notions of propriety and the world of appearances. The JA community could have been a wonderful place to grow up in, but when you are born a nail that sticks out, there is one inevitable fate awaiting you. At least that is how I felt at the time.

I grew up in the Baldwin Hills/Crenshaw district. I played Community Youth Council (CYC) little league baseball and basketball on the Tigers Team. Neither of my parents experienced the internment camps (my mom was born in

Hawai'i, and my dad was born in Los Angeles and raised in Japan). All of my family's close friends were of Japanese ancestry. We attended barbecues, community events, and festivals. We ate Japanese food, including the quintessentially JA treat: tricolored jello. My grandmother lived at Tokyo Towers in Little Tokyo so we often visited her there. My dad always impressed upon us that we should feel proud to be Japanese—"never colonized," he'd point out.

But beyond that, my family did not embrace traditional JA values. We didn't go to Japanese school. My parents were street smart and not political—certainly not progressive. My mom encouraged us to achieve proficiency in the kitchen and at the card table. We grew up in a working class neighborhood. Neither of my parents had gone to college, so there was no real expectation that we excel academically. We had no religious training or orientation. Looking back, I guess we were raised with Libertarian-ish values. To be sure, we weren't the model minority JAs.

My childhood was uneventful and stable. We had our struggles as a family. But mostly we stuck together. In a way, my secret kept me safe. Without particular needs or desires beyond the basics of food, love, and shelter, I seemed to be a kid always thinking about the needs of others. No close friends. No school age crushes that could be shared in any public way. Secretly, I battled loneliness and despair—all the while wearing a silly, ear to ear grin. "Look, I'm soooo happy!" it seemed to say.

From the age of 5, I absolutely knew that I liked boys and all of that marriage/love stuff that is supposed to happen between a man and woman did not apply to me. Still, I wrestled with my attraction to boys. If we were the praying type of family, I would have appealed to Almighty God to take these feelings away. Yet any resolve to exorcise my gayness was reversed at the sight of a shirtless Robert Conrad tied up and interrogated on an episode of *The Wild, Wild West*, or a boy only two years older than I with armpit hair shooting a basketball, or a buck naked full grown man in the locker room while at my swimming lessons. The vacillations between guilt and pleasure were akin to the tempering of steel, the making of a resilient sword. My gayness was more powerful than any prayer that could be imposed. My quixotic belief that I would someday fall in love with a man sustained me; it was a beacon of hope that lit the way forward despite all evidence that I existed in a world not made for me.

As silly as it sounds, I really believed that I was singular—that there were no other gay JA boys in the entire world. This distortion, as it turns out, is shared by many JA gay men that I have only recently met as a result of being involved with Okaeri. Of course, I saw images in the media of gay men, but many of those images were emasculating stereotypes, portrayals of moral degradation, or characters that end in tragedy, like in the movie *Brokeback Mountain*. Crucially, the paucity of positive images of gay Asian men contributed to my false belief that being Asian was not desirable, not sexy, not worthy, not even male.

I joined the Army on July 5, 1983 and was discharged within a year and a half. I was given the boot along with my first boyfriend Chris after another soldier caught us having sex in the barracks. Chris and I were both given a General Discharge Under Honorable Conditions. I had to call my parents from Fort Hood, Texas and explain to them why I was returning home prematurely and that I would be accompanied by my lover.

Chris and I started our gay life together. Though it was amidst the HIV/AIDS crisis, we lived in a little bubble of first love, removed from death, politics, and the shifts in society that led to the modern gay liberation movement. Chris and I joined a young men's rap group at the Gay and Lesbian Center. We started to form our chosen family of LGBTQ+ folk, access community resources, and learn about gay culture, gay history, and camp and drag as forms of resistance.

In 1992, I had the good fortune of meeting Dan—an academic and activist—through a personal ad in *Frontiers*—a local free rag distributed in gay bars. We dated for a year, during which I was initiated into developing a relationship with my psyche. Our intimacy was of both a caustic and tender nature, undergirded by the Jungian concept of the Shadow[1]. There was no standing on ceremony dating Dan, no inconvenience spared if it meant "processing" something. It sounds tedious and it often was, but somehow, it was invigorating. I really had no idea who I was and what made me tick.

Dan was my boyfriend, mentor, and guru. He guided me

---

1 "The Shadow," coined by Swiss psychologist Carl Jung, refers to an unconscious part of the psyche that is the repository of repressed thoughts, attitudes and feelings that people do not like to acknowledge. For an LGBTQ+ person, the Shadow may contain elements of self-loathing, fear of self, fear of sex, internalized homophobia, hatred, and jealousy of others, sado-masochistic fantasies, etc. In this sense, exploring the Shadow self can be part of a liberating reclamation of cast off parts.

through a process of self-discovery and introduced me to his therapist, Michael, whom I began to see shortly after, and met with every week for approximately 13 years. Even after breaking up, I continued relating with Dan weekly in a gay men's writing group that he hosted at his home. Therapy was a revelation, peeling away at layers of trauma and creating meaning out of suffering. Through dream analysis, I discovered that my inner world was full of monsters and angels, all enlisted in the self-actualizing potential of the mind to heal through a deft weaving of symbols and archetypes. In therapy, I learned that being gay was the most wonderful gift, but wrapped in a paradox: gay people don't have biological children but produce "children of the mind" through our contributions to society, as argued in Plato's *Symposium*. When my therapist introduced *shudo*—the pederastic traditions observed by Edo era *samurai*—my mind was blown. I was able to envision a bridge to my gay ancestors and feel a sense of gay Japanese pride. I started to see myself as a warrior. I mused that in feudal Japan, I might have been plucked from a monastery by a handsome *samurai* who would make me his *wakashu*, and usher me into manhood. Having this erotic mirror interrupted my fixed gaze on White gay men. Naturally, I started to see beautiful Asian men all around me.

As an outgrowth of therapy, I also got sober from alcohol. I admitted that I used alcohol to run away from my sexuality and to keep myself numb. Getting sober landed me in the gay recovery community where I met a loving sponsor and sobriety "sisters" who guided me through the 12 Steps.

Through Alcoholics Anonymous, I met and started dating Steve, who was also sober. For the first time in my gay life, I felt like a part of a community.

In 2003, I went to my parents' home, sat them down, pounded my fist on their dining table and told them that they were shitty parents. My father took it with cool levelheaded silence. My mom cried. I surmised that a gay warrior was better off with no parents. If you had suggested to me that just a decade later I would be planning a conference for *Nikkei* LGBTQ+ folk and their families and allies, and that it would be hosted at the Japanese American National Museum, I would have laughed.

I was a shameless evangelist of gay-centered therapy. When Chris, my first boyfriend, came over for the last time to visit Steve and me, I failed to see that he was saying goodbye to us. He kissed us on the forehead before sauntering out, like he was bestowing some kind of blessing. He committed suicide a month later. His note read, "I'm sorry to take the coward's way out." Gay life is not easy. Suicides, mental health issues, and addictions are not unfamiliar challenges; not as proof of gay pathology, but evidence of the corrosive effects of trauma that LGBTQ+ kids endure, often without intervention. All of the warrior training that I was engaged in seemed pointless when I could not save a friend that I loved.

Giving up alcohol opened up channels of erotic energy. I hit the gym and started going out to clubs and bars by myself. Prior to this period, I hated my Asian face, eyes, dick, and body because I had been conditioned to feel that way. Even personal ads blatantly stated, "NO FATS. NO FEMS.

NO ASIANS." Since I did not have ties to the *Nikkei* or Asian Pacific Islander community, I was vulnerable to succumbing to these messages. It didn't help that when I first came out at 19, I innocently assumed that I had finally arrived. It did not take long, however, before I realized how the gay male world was simply a microcosm of society and that all of society's "isms" were neatly reconstituted in the gay community with White gay men at the top of the pecking order. Gay men of color were either emasculated or fetishized to the point of being invisible.

When I finally got the nerve to enter a bathhouse, I stood in front of the attendant's window, paid, and was buzzed in. Still clothed, I walked around the labyrinthine space, a massive three story warehouse dimly lit and decorated with Hollywood memorabilia. I undressed, took a shower and donned a white towel and walked around again. There was one young Latino man, probably in his early twenties sitting on a bench at the top of the stairs. He was so beautiful. He had a trim body, fresh faded haircut, dark, deep set eyes, full lips, and smooth golden skin. I walked past him trying to make eye contact. He gave me a polite nod of acknowledgement. I kept walking. I ended up at the other side of the landing and pretended not to be watching him. "This is crazy!" I thought.

When there was no one around, I walked over to him and introduced myself. Befittingly his name was Angel. This was his first time at this bathhouse too. I told him that I found him beautiful. He thanked me. My body pulsed with desire. I also felt terrified of being rejected. But something that I was working on in therapy guided me to find the courage to pursue my Soul Figure—the man who approximates the image that resides on the altar of love in my psyche. The goal, as explained by my therapist, was not to seek to possess, but to be receptive to relating to an object of love as freely and courageously as possible. The goal was not to have sex with Angel, but to acknowledge how he made me feel. A rejection would not mean all the things that my inner critic would say. I asked Angel if it was ok if I sat next to him and he gestured that it was. I looked into his soulful eyes. After some small talk, I asked him if he wanted to come to my room. He said yes. I was probably close to 33 at the time and this was the first time that I approached another man for sex in such a direct way. Angel was hesitant at first but he returned my kisses and we ended up making out and jerking off together. It was so innocent and safe. I thanked him, cupped his handsome face in my hands, and told him to "please be safe."

As a gay JA man, I am proud of my sexual journey. The 2022 movie, *Fire Island* illustrates how sex in the gay male world is a form of currency, and is used to form relationships, transcend ethnic and class barriers, build networks, exclude certain groups, and in some cases advance a person's particular needs or goals. For me, sex was not just an affirmation of being desirable, but evidence in the face of virulent anti-Asian bias that I was not the piece of shit that I felt like and sociological proof that White A-list guys that would not give me the time of day in a bar had no problem being with me at a bathhouse. All of this begs the question, however, how much gratuitous sex does one need to have to prove a point? When I started taking my journals to the baths to reflect on my feelings and developments in therapy, I sensed that I was nearing the end of the experience of hooking up, and that the image of my Soul Figure was better left on the psychic altar, than projected onto mere mortal men. As I became more at peace with my body and identity, my psyche turned inward still deeper to other treasures. I ended up going back to college, completing a bachelor's degree and master's degree in preparation for being a psychotherapist. Therapy, I felt, had saved my life and opened up vistas of beauty, meaning, and possibility. I wanted to pay that forward to other LGBTQ+ folk.

Therapy, sobriety, and studying psychology eventually led me to reunite with my family. I realized that it would be hypocritical of me to become a therapist when I had unfinished business with them. Ten years had elapsed since I slammed my fist on the table and told them that they were shitty parents. They were now in their late 60s/early 70s. On the day that I met with my parents and siblings for our reunion, my dad proclaimed, "Look Annie, our prodigal son has returned!" How odd it was to see them older. What impressed me most was how happy my mom seemed. She was not pining away for me. In fact, she had thrived in my absence! Though she admitted to missing me, ever the pragmatist, she clearly accepted my decision to leave the family and focused on creating her own happiness.

Before dinner, my dad got up from the dining table. He returned with a Native American talking stick. He placed it on the table saying, "This is how we are going to do this. The person with the stick talks." When it was my turn to hold the stick, I told my parents that I missed my family, that it was hard to be without a family, but in their absence I had created a chosen family of friends who supported me through the darkest days of my addictions, the initial arcs of therapy, and the loss of Chris. My chosen family encouraged me to go back to school and supported me reconnecting with my biological family.

In 2012, I was completing my master's degree in clinical psychology at Antioch University and interning at an LGBTQ+ Youth Counseling Center, COLORS, that provided free psychotherapy to young people, couples, and adults. The supervisors at COLORS often invited guest speakers and trainers. One day, my fellow interns and I were informed that two special guests would be speaking. Nothing more was explained. As we got settled in our seats around a big conference table, an older Asian woman and a young Asian guy walked in. The woman's name was Marsha Aizumi and the young person accompanying her was her son, Aiden. They had come to share their coming out stories and experiences as a Japanese American mother and trans son. In that next hour and a half, as Marsha described the journey of a mother who was lost, did not know who to turn to, was afraid of being judged by her community and church, and most poignantly, deeply concerned that her son would not survive the challenges posed by transitioning and find love of his own, I felt something inside of me crack. It felt like the fear and hurt of my childhood that had crystallized inside of me had burst into hundreds of tiny jagged pieces that were tearing me up from the inside. I heard a Japanese American mother say the words I did not know I longed to hear from my own mother. I heard her say, "I'm sorry that I caused you to suffer. I'm sorry that I did not know how to support you."

Anyone reading this will know that meeting Marsha and Aiden turned out to be another turning point in my life and the starting point for my journey back to my birth community (and Okaeri)—yet another improbability amongst many unforeseen encounters with angels.

FINDING MY WAY HOME
Alden M. Hayashi

When I was in my twenties, struggling to find my way through life, I very much identified as a gay man. At the time, being Japanese American was more like a minor footnote of my existence, much to the considerable consternation of my *Nisei* parents. My father, who was then president of the Honolulu Hiroshima *Kenjinkai*, must have been particularly disappointed that I showed so little interest in my ethnic and cultural heritage.

I think that my strong identification with being gay had much to do with the AIDS epidemic. As a young gay man in the 1980s, I felt so vulnerable, with close friends becoming gravely ill and anti-gay vitriol intensifying throughout those terrible years. Things came to a head when my cousin Joey, a Broadway actor, was stricken with HIV. Joey was like my

"Auntie Mame"—he taught me to enjoy life and to accept (and, more importantly, to forgive) myself for being gay. I am the man I am today because of him and, when he died a slow, agonizing death from AIDS-related complications in 1987, I was devastated. My grief became all the more acute because I couldn't talk openly to my parents about their nephew Joey, and what he had meant to me and how he had helped me to come out. My *Sansei* cousins and I had to be careful what we said in front of our *Nisei* relatives, because the last thing we wanted to do was add to the pain of Joey's parents.

I also had friends who died horrible, excruciating deaths from AIDS and I couldn't talk to my parents about any of that either. I was living in Boston and they were living in Honolulu, where I was born and raised, and all our conversations over the phone tended to stick to "safe" topics like the weather, the Red Sox, and updates about relatives— what cousin was getting married or having babies, etc. Forget about any discussion of safe sex. When it came to condom usage, my mother would only say, "I hope you're not doing anything stupid out there."

Today, decades later, I feel much more threatened as an Asian American, more likely to be assaulted by racists than by gay bashers. Living in Boston, I now make sure that my cell phone is adequately charged whenever I leave my apartment, just in case I might need to record some racist incident so that I'll have video proof. I've also become increasingly aware of subtle things. The other month I was walking around the Back Bay neighborhood of Boston when I noticed a Chinese woman in the distance trying to figure out how the new parking meters work. She was standing there in frustration as a number of pedestrians (all white) walked by her. Then, as soon as she could make out my face, she came rushing toward me, motioning that she needed help. She didn't speak much English at all, and I can't speak a word of Mandarin, but somehow we were able to communicate. After I had showed her how to use her credit card to pay the meter, she was so grateful, effusively thanking me several times. Her gratitude was touching yet it also made me sad that she didn't feel comfortable approaching anyone but a fellow Asian.

All this has led to a huge shift in how I perceive myself: I now feel that my fundamental identity is that of a Japanese American who happens to be gay, rather than a gay man who happens to be Japanese American. Ironically, it was my being gay that initially led me to turn away from the Japanese American community. I was so afraid to be judged by the *Issei* and *Nisei* generations. In their eyes, I thought I had fallen far short of the "model minority" ideal, and I wanted to flee the shame I felt. Interestingly, I don't think that my parents' anti-gay prejudices came from any entrenched religious or moral objections. I think it was more of a "what will the neighbors think" anxiety: they were afraid that somehow my homosexuality would bring community shame through the front door of their home. I believe that my parents, who are now both deceased, regretted that that attitude kept them at arm's distance from me when I was in my twenties, thirties, and even early forties. We wasted so much time—time that can never be recovered. But thankfully we were able to reconnect with each other and have deep, meaningful conversations in their twilight years.

As I now reflect on things, I am so grateful to have lived long enough to experience my life having come full circle, with Japanese Americans, especially the *Yonsei* and *Gosei* generations, increasingly embracing all of the beautiful diversity in our community. I have become all the more proud of my Japanese heritage, and my voice feels so included and truly embraced as part of the rich *Nikkei* landscape. And somewhere up there, I believe my *Nisei* parents are smiling, knowing that, after a long journey with numerous detours, I was able to find my way home again as a Japanese American. Whenever I left my parents' house in Honolulu to return to the mainland, they would tell me, "Your home will always be waiting here for you, *always*." It's taken me decades to realize that they were more right than ever I could have imagined.

Being a gender nonconforming Japanese American,

I have been working on decolonizing

world. Pr... r expans...

pro-queer, pro-...ing class... ndi...

determination, p... ck sol... r.

This is me.

ムたち一人一...の中

輝いている...で...

In her hom... ate chicke...

makizushi a... er kitchen tabl...

She guided... d with her...

howed m... w... se the wo...

ush fo... hi-e... er hom...

to and an...

pride for family, and was able

mind of the confusing and self-har...

05

WHERE WE FIND HOME

MY ALOHA
Jill Togawa

When I was working on the last piece I intended to create as a Bay Area resident, I struggled with my decision to move home again after spending more than half my adult life always living at a distance. It was a giant step for me—maybe one I could not take after all. Then one day in the studio, I quieted enough, and I could hear everything. I knew the return was an announcement of *okaeri* to myself, and I could carry my life's résumé of all I had experienced since I had left O'ahu as a young adult. At 21 I had had no name for the recurring feelings that pulled at me more and more insistently. I came out in New York, moved to the San Francisco Bay area, and found community first with other API sisters, then other artists, BIPOC folks, and *sangha* with queer Buddhists of color. Gratitude smooths the path that delivered me back to my place, with all parts accounted for, for the first time.

My Aloha
(from Purple Moon Dance Project's 'Uhane')

My body says 'go home'....

Learn to breathe warm air again,

Unfurl.

My soul says 'It's time now,

Close a door

Open the windows

Let the love in.

Sit beside your father,

Ask him to tell you his stories,

For the last time.

Tell your mother you love her

Bring your child to her

Walk to her whenever you can.

Stop searching

Feel the *anuhea*

Listen to its   *cool*   *silence.*

FINDING PRIDE IN FARGO

Reiko Yokota Barnett

In 2000, my family moved from Texas to the upper
Midwest state of North Dakota. I rarely saw anyone who
looked like me, a Japanese American. I worried about what my
children would experience in school, being Asian American in
a predominantly white community. I was pleasantly surprised
when those worries were diminished in what I came to know
as "Midwestern nice." What that meant was that people were
so polite and nice, and they accepted me "invisibly." People
asked where I was from, and when I responded, "Texas,"
they didn't ask any further questions. I was assimilating and
blending into life in the Midwest, but there was no one to
share my feelings or outlook on life from an Asian lens. North
Dakota was just starting to become more racially diverse
as immigrants were settling into the state, but the Asian

community remained small, and the Japanese community was even smaller. After a year of living here, I was introduced to some Japanese women, and we held bimonthly luncheons, known as JLL—Japanese Ladies Luncheon. This was my only opportunity to speak Japanese and have conversations that related to anything Japanese. But, while I was able to connect with other Japanese living in our city, my children could not, and had to navigate their identities alone.

Both of my children had mostly positive experiences in school. They did well academically, but with added comments of "because they are Asian." They participated in many extracurricular activities and thrived in leadership roles. What I didn't know as a mom was how they related to their peers. I recall a time when I made cupcakes in an ice cream cone for my daughter's birthday, which she took to school. When I asked if her classmates liked her cupcakes, she shook her head and said, "Mom, you need to come talk to my class because everyone thought they were Japanese!" My son played on an intramural soccer team in high school, and one day he came home with a shirt that had all their nicknames on it. His name was Kung Fu Panda. When I asked about it, he said that was the name his teammates gave him. I thought to myself, that is not the same culture, and just not OK. These are stories of my children being seen, but not for who they truly are.

My daughter's main criteria for college was to move away as far as possible. Perhaps this was her way of hoping to find a place where she could be seen in a way North Dakota could never offer. I thought it was her independent streak that she was displaying, especially as it coincided with the time my former husband and I worked through a difficult divorce. My daughter had always shown typical first born traits so when she said she wanted to move to Los Angeles after her college graduation in 2015, I supported her decision even though she didn't have a job lined up. She absolutely loved living in LA and made life work for her, starting with various part time jobs which eventually led to a successful career in the media world.

In 2017, my sister's family and mine traveled to celebrate Christmas together. It was then that my daughter announced to everyone that she liked men and women and was in a relationship with a woman. Immediately, my family embraced her, but internally, I was confused. I knew gay people, but no one in my close circle of friends. I didn't understand the layers of what being bisexual meant. I also had a tinge of disappointment that I was informed at the same time as everyone else, and felt that my role as her mom wasn't important. Suddenly, I was a mom to a child that I didn't know how to continue to parent. I felt clueless.

I had a lot of questions, so I started with a private breakfast with her the next morning. I first apologized for anything I had said during her years at home that may have confused or invalidated who she was. I wanted to know when and how did she know? I am grateful for her openness in sharing, teaching me, and most of all, inviting me into her life. What I have come to learn is that it isn't about me, but about her journey towards coming out and becoming her authentic self.

When I returned to North Dakota after that Christmas, I felt a heaviness inside, carrying this information, but not understanding my role. I looked up support groups such as PFLAG, but there were none in Fargo. I had to figure this out on my own. I wondered how to respond when people asked how she was doing—do I out my daughter? She had given me permission to share but I wasn't sure how. While it's hard to admit now that my first attempts were delivered with a pause, then a lowered voice that she identified as queer and was in a relationship with a woman, the most common response I received was "That's Ok, as long as she's happy." I realized how that Midwestern nice comment really cut deeply. It was separating "them"—church-going, white, conservative traditional families—from "me."

My daughter continues to help me grow in my understanding, acceptance, and inclusivity. When she invited me to participate in my first Okaeri conference (virtually), I was in awe of everyone who spoke and shared their story. For the first time in my adult years, I saw a mirror on my Zoom screen of other Japanese Americans with similar experiences, and as the speakers spoke from their hearts, I felt a deep connection. That experience has led me to speak with a louder voice in this Midwestern nice community.

I recently spoke to a friend whom I hadn't seen for well over 10 years. As we talked about our children and she shared that one of her children was transitioning, I responded with "Isn't it beautiful when our children find themselves to become their authentic self?" She was stunned by my response as I shared my own journey as a parent of an LGBTQ+ child.

In the summer of 2022, there was a weeklong celebration of events in Fargo for Gay Pride Week. I rode my bike downtown by myself. What a surprise and joy it was to see the sheer number of people both in the parade and along the route as spectators. It was such a beautiful sight to see such diverse people of all ages, colors, and identities. Parents and friends of LGBTQ+ people held signs and wore shirts with messages of love and support. Although I was happy and proud of how far my community has grown in inclusivity, I felt alone and sad that I was experiencing this without my daughter.

I will be moving away from this community next year when I retire to a warmer climate near a beach. In 2023, my daughter Mia planned a trip to come help me downsize and clean out my house in preparation, and we discovered that her trip coincidentally was during Fargo Pride Week! My son and his girlfriend also joined us at the Pride Block Party where hundreds of people gathered for a drag show performance. It was exciting to stand side by side with my children and cheer at the Pride Parade. My family hanging out together at this event is something I could not have imagined in my past. I realized that while our lives do not unfold in a predictable manner, living and celebrating in the present is where I want to be. It is my joy and privilege to share how I celebrate every fiber of who my children are and their place in our world.

SOFTENING STEEL
Mia Barnett

The first time I became ashamed of my ethnicity was during a backyard soccer game the summer after second grade. Prior to this, I loved my Japanese heritage and always proudly declared that I was half Japanese if it ever came up in conversation. But during that soccer game, the two girls that I had been playing with all summer called me over and told me that they were going to go home and didn't want to play with me anymore because I was Black. I'm not Black, and in retrospect, perhaps their parents were spewing anti-Black, white supremacist rhetoric and these seven-year-olds got confused. But the message to me was clear: they no longer wanted to be friends with me because I wasn't white like them.

I was devastated. I ran inside, sobbing. I had just moved to Fargo, North Dakota one year prior and these two girls were among my only friends. I told my mom what happened and she responded by encouraging me to brush it off and return to playing with them. I'm not resentful of my mom for reacting in this way—I'm sure she was thinking about how hard I had tried to make friends and didn't want me to feel alone. But I internalized something that day: it was okay for people to dislike me for who I was, and it was my job to not let it bother me.

I didn't ever play with those girls again, and over time, I steeled my heart. I hated how hurt I was by what those girls said, and I was determined to never let anyone make me feel that way again. During my freshman year of high school, I laughed off comments about how it made sense I was good at math because I was Asian. I pretended I didn't care when my classmates planned a "Hug An Asian Day" sophomore year, my only resistance being ducking away from unwanted hugs as me and the other five Asian students were harassed all day. At my part-time job at Blockbuster, I would fire back canned responses to the frequent questions from customers of "where are you from?" and "what are you?" I stopped sharing that I was Japanese, and since I am mixed, white-passing, and have a non-Japanese last name, I was able to hide my ethnicity most of the time. This felt safe.

Reflecting on my high school years is painful. I was deeply unhappy and terrified of being vulnerable, and I lacked the language and resources to articulate this or even realize what I was going through. Because I was constantly living in survival mode, I wasn't able to explore my queerness either. Constantly building up walls left little energy for introspection. I thought about my sexual orientation, but only in fleeting moments, and convinced myself that there was no way I could be gay because I didn't want to cut my hair short or wear a suit to my wedding (of course, my only frame of reference for queerness being Ellen DeGeneres). Plus, I knew that I at least liked boys so I felt there was no need to really explore further than that because I could just marry a man and probably be happy.

Going to college felt like my ticket out of the place that had made me so miserable, so I only looked at colleges on the east coast, trying to get as far away from Fargo as possible. My parents were sad that I wanted to go so far and tried to convince me to choose some place closer, but that didn't feel good enough to me. I wanted to meet people who thought differently than those I grew up around, and going far away felt like it would give me the best chance of meeting those types of people. After receiving a diversity scholarship (which made me feel guilty for denying my heritage until it became financially prudent for me to claim it), I decided to attend Kenyon College in Ohio.

I viewed college as the chance for me to reinvent myself. I signed up for a Japanese class right away, and made my first-ever Japanese American friend. She was from Los Angeles and would tell me stories of attending a predominantly Japanese high school in the South Bay, and I was fascinated. I couldn't imagine not being in the minority in any space I was in, because although Kenyon was much more diverse than my high school, it was still predominantly white. At Kenyon I also met a new type of person: rich, white, coastal kids. I was on a scholarship for minority students and financial aid, and it shocked me that over half of my classmates had families who were able to just pay the $60,000 tuition out of pocket. I felt ashamed to share that my mother was a teacher and my father worked at WalMart, while my classmates' parents had huge law firms in New York City or ran The Washington Post. I had years of practice steeling myself from feeling shame, so it was easy for me to assimilate and pretend I was just like my peers. And when my parents went through a messy divorce that I struggled with, the goal of reinventing myself during college was replaced with the familiar and comfortable survival mode.

During spring break of my senior year, my friend from Los Angeles invited me to come home with her. I visited LA for the very first time and walked around Little Tokyo in awe. I couldn't believe that not only was there a neighborhood dedicated to Japanese culture, but that it was a community with Japanese people. I knew I wanted to be back in LA as soon as possible, and I moved there a couple months after graduation.

Though I arrived only knowing my roommates, I was so excited about the possibilities of a new city—a city filled with Asian people and communities and neighborhoods—that I wasn't nervous at all. No one stared at me in public. No one asked me where I was from, like really from. It didn't take long for me to feel at home.

After a year of working low-paying assistant jobs and nannying on the weekends, I landed a job at BuzzFeed, a tech and media company that was churning out viral videos like "If Men Were Disney Princesses" and "14 Sex Facts You

Won't Believe Are True." Working at BuzzFeed was the most fun I'd ever had at a job. You'd be working on a project and suddenly an office-wide message would be sent asking for any volunteers to answer geography questions while drunk or sample international snacks for a video. A lot of the content we worked on had to do with identity, and thus, my coworkers were diverse. Many were also millennial LA transplants looking for friends, so I quickly connected with my coworkers. There was a reason we all joked that work was actually just "BuzzFeed High."

It was my job to quality check all of the BuzzFeed videos, and seeing how open my friends were about their identities, about coming out, and about being queer gave me so much courage. (There's a conversation to be had about why they felt they had to be so open to get views on their videos, but that's a conversation for another day.) Not only did I now have a community of Asian people, but queer Asian people. A new friend started inviting me to Little Tokyo community events, and I felt like I was a part of the Japanese American community in LA that I had been so excited to discover on my initial trip in college. It was during this time that I began to discover parts of my identity that I had been unwilling or unable to look into back in high school and college. I met my partner at work, came out to most of my friends, and then came out to my family.

It was difficult for me to work through feelings of shame about coming out at 25 years old. There are, of course, people who come out at all stages of life, and plenty that come out after 25. I didn't judge those people but experienced a lot of shame about my own timeline. For some reason, I couldn't extend the same compassion I felt about others to myself. Looking back, I think the shame was rooted in jealousy for people who came out in high school and college and were able to openly explore their identities. They seemed to be so much more confident and comfortable while I was just a baby queer. While coming out was freeing, I still felt like I had somehow done it "wrong."

It was around this time that I realized I needed to work on my mental health. It was as if there were layers to myself buried so far beneath my survival mechanisms that I barely noticed they were there. I felt like I had figured out what being Japanese American meant for me, which then allowed me to explore my queerness. Coming out subsequently allowed me to admit to myself that I needed help. I started to see a therapist who diagnosed me with anxiety and depression. She also diagnosed me with Obsessive Compulsive Disorder (OCD) but didn't have experience treating it. I decided to seek out a therapist who specializes in OCD treatment and learned that my previous therapist had been using methods that actually worsened my OCD. I began intensive treatment, and after two years, I felt like I was in a healthy enough place to take a break from therapy. Reaching the milestone of finishing treatment felt like placing the final piece in the puzzle of myself. I felt at peace.

Whenever people ask me if I'd ever leave Los Angeles (which is a question I often get and I don't know why), I say that it would be really difficult to leave the community I've found here. My community gave me the space and permission to finally let down my walls. To finally have all of the different parts of my identity reflected in the people I was around showed me what my life could be. It let me access parts of myself that, as an adolescent, I was prepared to never explore.

I recently returned to Fargo to help my mom prepare to move and discovered that my trip coincided with Fargo Pride. I was excited to see what Pride was like in Fargo, to see how far my community had come since I had last lived there 12 years prior. It was beautiful to see how supportive the community was, but I was surprised that it didn't really feel like my community. I was happy for queer and trans Fargoans, but I no longer count myself as one of them. Instead, the overwhelming feeling I had was pride for my younger self. I was so proud of her for choosing to be brave: brave enough to move away from home, brave enough to come out, brave enough to seek treatment. I never felt brave during any stage of my life, but I've realized that bravery is more of an action than a feeling.

Standing in the rain watching the colorful floats roll by, I picture that second grader from the soccer game all those years back next to me, and I smile. I squeeze her hand and tell her, "You've got this."

THE SHAPE OF OKAERI
Momo Hoshi

Having been born and raised in San Diego, I assumed that the perpetually sunny perfection of a city would always be my one and only "home." However, this one-dimensional understanding of "home" started to splinter when I went to college, and my family moved to Northern California around the same time. On one hand, I was delighted that "home" would be moving with me. It grounded me to know that the doors I walk through to hear that familiar exchange—"お帰り (okaeri)!" "ただいま (tadaima)"—would be just a 20 minute drive from my college dorm.

At the same time, San Diego started to feel less like home, and more like a distant friend that I used to know. During winter breaks in undergrad, my high school friends would all return to San Diego from their respective colleges. Our group chat would blow up with plans to get boba, compare first semester experiences, and spill new tea. All the while, I would linger in the background, afraid to break the bubbled up anticipation with my melancholy.

These feelings of ungroundedness continued to percolate throughout my college years, and eventually burst open when my family moved back to Japan the year I graduated from college. Of course I was grateful that my parents, especially my mom, would finally get the chance to return to her own "home" after 30 years of raising her children in a foreign land that she never ended up finding ease in. I was excited for this next chapter of their lives. Simultaneously, "*okaeri*" would suddenly become very much out of reach for me, I felt. Especially in a family where we don't put our love and appreciation into straightforward words, the feeling of "*okaeri*" has always lived in the little things—my mom making me my favorite *karaage* every time I would stop by for dinner, my childhood cat pretending to not like the attention I gave him, my dad unpromptedly telling me about the music he'd been listening to lately. Those small pockets of "*okaeri*" were suddenly so much further from me than I'd ever experienced.

In those moments that feel saturated with solitude, my proverbial beacon of light is a concept that both the Asian American and queer & trans communities taught me and continue to remind me of each day: family can be a choice, and home can be a feeling. I distinctly remember the term "chosen family" being introduced to me during college, as I gingerly stepped into more queer spaces my junior year as a way to explore my own gender and sexual identities. Despite being still so unsure of the shape of my own queerness, I was welcomed with open arms and no need for labels or self-justifications. The queer community simultaneously tore down the rigid walls that contained so many of the ideologies I had grown up assuming as immutable truths—ideas about gender, sexuality, family, identities, self-discovery journeys, life paths, etc.—while also giving me new, more sustainable building blocks with which to create the foundations that uphold the expansive understandings of family and community I am so thankful to have today. I now know that there are no limitations on who can be family, what can be home, and how abundantly we can be surrounded by the warmth of "coming home."

Because these communities have welcomed and celebrated me for the full extent of who I am and the multitudes I contain, I have also learned how to come home to myself, in a way. "*Okaeri*" has now been liberated beyond any four walls, beyond zip codes, beyond any single person, place, or thing. Instead, "*okaeri*" is dynamic, aglow, and perpetually in flight in each and every one of us.

「お帰り」の形
星桃

　南カリフォルニアのサンディエゴで生まれ育った私は、常に太陽が降り注ぐあの青空の街が唯一の「故郷」だと一生感じるだろうと思い込んでいた。しかし、大学に進学する頃から「故郷」に対するその一面的な理解が崩れ始めた。ちょうどその頃、両親も一緒に北カリフォルニアに移住した。「故郷」が一緒に来てくれたみたいで、ある意味嬉しかった。ほんの20分運転すれば、いつもの「お帰り」、「ただいま」がある。そう考えただけでホッとした。

　同時に、サンディエゴという街を故郷というよりは、どんどん遠い昔の友人のように感じ始めた。大学の冬休みになると、高校時代の友達は皆、それぞれの大学からサンディエゴへ帰って行った。みんなはグループチャットで予定を立てる。一緒にお茶しよう、お互いの大学一学期目の経験について語り合おう、最近の噂話をしよう、と。その溢れるようなワクワク感に水を差さぬよう、私は何も言わずに一人で切なさを抱えた。

　この不安な気持ちは大学時代ずっと続いた。大学を卒業した年に両親が日本に帰る決断をした時、とうとう不安が動揺に変わった。もちろん、

30年間アメリカで子育てを頑張ってくれた母親が、やっと母国に帰れる事に対しては感謝の気持ちしかない。父と母が人生の次の一歩を踏み出した事は祝うべきことだ。だがその反面、私にとってはいきなり「お帰り」が手の届かない所にいってしまう、そう感じたのだった。私の家族では、愛情や感謝の気持ちは言葉ではなく、行動で表す。私が夕飯を食べに家へ帰ると必ず大好物の唐揚げを作ってくれる母、素直に構って欲しいとは言えない愛猫、聞いてもいないのに最近聴いている音楽について語り出す父。ささやかな「お帰り」が、突然今までよりずっと遠くなってしまう。

けれど、儚さや寂しさの中唯一助けになるのが、大学時代にアジア系アメリカ人コミュニティーやクィア・トランズコミュニティーから教わった事である。家族は選べる、そして故郷は場所に限らず、フィーリングでもある。大学 3 年目、性自認や性的指向などの自分のアイデンティティーを理解したく、少しずつクィア・コミュニティーのイベントなどに参加し始めた。その頃、chosen family、「自分が選んだ家族」という言葉を初めて耳にした。自分ですら自分がクィアなのか何なのか確かでない中、コミュニティーは私を歓迎してくれた。ジェンダーやセクシャリティー、家族やアイデンティティー、自分探しの旅の形や人生の歩み方などについての凝り固まった考え方から解放されたのも、クィアコミュニティーのおかげだ。家族やコミュニティーについて、今までより豊かな思想の土台を創り上げる事ができた。その経験があったからこそ、誰と家族になり、どこを故郷と感じ、どれだけ温かく「お帰り」に包まれるか、そういったことに限りは無いという事を知った。

コミュニティーに歓迎され、私の全てを受け入れてもらえた経験があるからこそ、ある意味自分に帰る事もできた。「お帰り」という気持ちは住所や一定の場所には限られることなく、場所や物や人をも越えた物である。「お帰り」は私たち一人一人の中で常に変化しながら、躍動感溢れ、輝いているものである。

THIS IS ME
eri oura

My name is eri oura.

In Japanese, *eri* means blessed one, and *oura* means big water.

I am a gender nonconforming, transgender *Sansei* person.

It took me 29 years to figure out my gender didn't fit in the gender binary. I know it will continue to evolve as I get to know myself more.

I grew up in Hawai'i with my *Nisei* dad, who had assimilated to American standards of existence for survival. For him, many things existed in binaries—good or bad, work hard or be lazy, satisfactory or unsatisfactory, male or female, statehood or remain a territory, straight or gay. Growing up with these values bound up in binaries made it so hard for me to consider myself outside of all of these things.

In my mid-20s, I found myself going really hard towards

efforts to demilitarize these sacred islands. That meant I stood and acted in solidarity with the indigenous people, *Kanaka ʻŌiwi*, who taught me about seeing the world outside of the American colonial and imperial mindset. For example, *Māhū*, a Hawaiian word that refers to LGBTQ+ folks, presented a concept that evolved in my understanding of the word. At the time, I noticed that many *māhū* folks subscribed to identifying within the gender binary too. Doing everything to "pass" as the gender they identified with most.

As someone assigned female at birth, I knew I never wanted to be a man. I think I developed some early onset misandry because of my experiences as the youngest girl in my family. I experienced men as mostly entitled, dominating, violent, and never giving women or other gendered folks enough credit.

When I decided to leave Hawaiʻi at age 28, I knew it was because I wanted to grow—to expand my capacity for all the possibilities this universe has to offer! As much as I loved being in Hawaiʻi, I knew it was time to allow myself to immerse in a setting where I could be myself with less care for other people's judgements. In a place where I could be my queerest self. Some place where there are more opportunities economically and socially to free myself from the limitations of my island home.

Moving to Oakland, CA, I had no idea what was waiting for me, but I knew that I needed to take this leap. The San Francisco Bay Area is known for its queer friendly culture and I felt that everytime I had visited before. My brother had moved there in 2006, and I visited him several times before moving to Oakland.

When I finally got there, I moved into a collectively run home for QTBIPOC in East Oakland (Oakland Sustaining Ourselves Locally) that rocked my world. Oakland SOL was made up of other community organizers, who, like me, were on a mission to make bold statements about existing in our bodies as queer and trans people of color and shifting the narratives away from the binaries that were meant to limit us, to suppress who we really are: other dimensional beings that cannot be contained by limited and oppressive binaries.

My housemates were also versed in talking about racial politics in a way that honored Black folks' experiences on Turtle Island. We would take to the streets every time there was a call to action from our community. This was really powerful for me to experience because there weren't many Black folks in Hawai'i when I was growing up. Most Black folks in Hawai'i were part of the military or university institutions, institutions that offer some privileges that local folks outside of those institutions didn't have access to. It has been painful and powerful for me to witness the structural and day-to-day violence that Black folks experience on Turtle Island. I would compare these experiences of violence to that of indigenous Pacific Islander folks' experiences back in Hawai'i, especially newer refugees like Micronesians.

Being a gender nonconforming Japanese American, I have been working on decolonizing my own narratives to match my political understanding of the world. Pro-gender expansive, pro-trans, pro-queer, pro-working class, pro-indigenous self-determination, pro-Black solidarity.

This is me.

FINDING COMMUNITY, BUILDING COMMUNITY

Jessica Miyeko Kawamura

I learned the phrase *okaeri* when I was introduced to my host mother during a semester abroad in Japan. When I arrived home after a long bus and train ride, I was to unlock the door and announce myself, saying "*Tadaima!*" In response, my host mom would reply, "*Okaeri!*" Welcome home.

Nearly twenty years have passed since then. I have spent almost all of my adult life far away from where I was born and raised in Berkeley, California. I spent my twenties on the East Coast, and my thirties living in Atlanta and now outside Honolulu.

Over the course of this time, my sense of self has grown and changed, both in terms of my identity as a Japanese American and as a queer person.

My childhood and teenage years were deeply shaped

by my experiences growing up in the Japanese American community in Berkeley and the East Bay. Like many *Yonsei* millennials, I grew up playing basketball, attending Japanese American summer school, and participating in *mochitsuki* and *obon* with the local Buddhist community. In high school, I was the youth representative on the board of the local chapter of the Japanese American Citizens League and participated in the Japanese American Cultural and Community Center of Northern California's basketball exchange program. In college, I was part of the Nikkei Community Internship Program, serving in San Francisco's Japantown.

For me, being Japanese American had always meant being part of the community. It was where I found my sense of self and my purpose in life. As the granddaughter of a camp survivor, I felt a call to serve the community and work for racial justice.

What was perhaps unique about my upbringing in Berkeley is my experience growing up in a historic Japanese American church as well as a progressive social and political context. More so than any of the Japanese American community activities I participated in, the most meaningful for me was our family's spiritual home at Berkeley Methodist United Church. My very favorite time of year was in May when we would have our church bazaar. I loved learning to cook curry and sushi and talk with the *Nisei* women in the congregation. More than anywhere else, our little historic Japanese American church felt like home.

When I moved away for college and then for work, I had to find community wherever I lived. On the East Coast, I was not near large communities of *Sansei* and *Yonsei*. In Washington, D.C. and New York City, I surrounded myself with other Asian American young professionals who shared my passion for public service and racial justice.

I also sought out spiritual community. In New York City, I landed at a progressive United Methodist congregation called The Church of the Village. Where I once had experienced love and support from *Nisei* women, I received care from middle aged white, black, and Latinx church members, many of whom were queer. Perhaps ironically, my first experience of intergenerational queer community was in the church.

My experience of loving community was so meaningful, that at age 30, I decided that I would quit my job and become a pastor serving historic Japanese American churches. I yearned for the sense of belonging that I felt as a youth, and envisioned that I would help to steward and care for faith communities like the one I grew up in. I was going to go home.

That was nearly eight years ago. If there is anything I have learned on my journey, it is that we never quite go home to the place where we came from. Over time, we change and so do the places that we remember.

As time has passed, I have grown in my understanding and acceptance of my queerness. I have learned to navigate the experience of passing as straight, faced some of my own internalized homophobia, and continued to seek out LGBTQ+ community. For me, these experiences have been ones of continually coming home to myself and who I am becoming.

My understanding of my *Yonsei* identity has also changed. Studying at a United Methodist seminary alongside Black and South Korean students led me to challenge my own racial privilege and the heaviness that can come with identifying as Japanese. Encountering queer and trans Christians from the South taught me about the harm being done to LGBTQ+ people by the Church and the reality of what is at stake in our fight for inclusion.

It turns out that I never returned back home. I ended up being assigned to a church in Hawaiʻi instead of California. I spent four and a half years pastoring a racially mixed congregation of Japanese, Filipino, Okinawan, Samoan, white, and hapa folks. In Hawaiʻi, unlike where I grew up, many of the people here do not particularly identify as Japanese or Asian American. I worked with the congregation through the process of becoming a formally LGBTQ+ affirming church. We did outreach to the queer and trans community in a context where conservative Christianity continues to cause immense harm. My journey, which is ongoing, has been isolating and scary, as well as life-changing and transformative.

Where do we find home as queer Japanese Americans? For so many of us, there is no going back. For some, our education and work have taken us far from home. Others have been rejected by our biological families and home communities. And for many of us, the Japanese American communities that we grew up in simply do not exist the way they did before. Our *Nisei* camp survivors have almost all passed away, and the institutions that they built struggle to survive.

Although I am thousands of miles away, I am heartened by the work of Okaeri and other next generation Japanese American organizations, many led by queer people. And, I continue to dream here in Hawai'i about the ways that we can build queer community for people here. We may not be going back, but we are always coming home and building home anew.

CHARTING SHAME AND SILENCE:
TRANSFORMING INTO RADICAL SOFTNESS AND SELF-CELEBRATION

Joseph Tsuboi

I felt confused and frustrated growing up. These feelings manifested more outwardly in high school—a time of deep insecurity—when I longed to fit in socially and match the uniqueness and intellectual skill of my peers. I did not know how to come into my own and fully embrace my differences as mixed-race, Asian American, and queer. Instead I felt pressured to fit in with my peers and perform well academically, living up to my parents' expectations and multiple degrees. Unfortunately, these familial pressures stifled my initial processes of coming out and they prevented me from being able to embrace each of my beautiful identities.

I did not grow up with any Japanese American cousins or close family my age with whom I could find some similarity. My uncle—my father's older brother—never married nor had children, and committed his adult life to caring for my widowed grandmother. I believe this to be an intergenerational product of the incarceration and their lifelong grieving of my grandfather's premature death. Both my uncle and dad responded to their family's post-war efforts to "recover" through a devotion to individualistic capitalism and financial gain. Nowadays, my sister and I—representing the next generation—have inherited a set of confusing and binding expectations. While our family has encouraged independence and progress in careers of our choice, it often feels risky to step out of Japanese American terms of success for fear of losing it all again.

Similarly, I did not see and was not exposed to models of queer Asian Americans growing up. I did not know it was okay to embrace multiple identities or that it was okay to step out of the known ways of relationship-building. Though I saw my mixed-race family as "different" than monoracial family contexts, I still felt my parents' investment in heteronormative gender roles: my white mother bearing and expressing many emotions, my Japanese American father suturing himself up to perform "good hard worker" and role model. Following psychologist Donna Nagata's research on the *Sansei* generation, I see how my father's fixation on financial wealth accumulation, social standing, and gender performance were selfless acts to try to erase his parents' incarceration-related traumas. Carried onto my generation, these markers of assimilation have been repeated—I believe out of fear—as means to "protect" me from what my father's generation had to go through. Yet, to me, these "protections" have greatly impacted the possibilities of embracing a fuller embrace and expression of my gender and queerness, as I learned to abide by these models and harden up the softer pieces of me.

In these difficult moments of isolation, I wish someone could have seen me and my insecurities and let me know that it would be okay. It is not to say I did not feel love or provision growing up; in fact, I miss dearly those shared unspoken moments, such as spending a lot of time in the car with my mom being chauffeured to sports practices and singing along to her array of music. What I craved was someone or something to break through what I was feeling even when I did not know what I may have needed. I'm also not fully sure how my folks would have better addressed my self-loathing and perhaps it was easier for them to suggest their routine practices of "wellness": again, diligence in school and other merit-based activities. Recently, I've tried to find greater appreciation of these intentions, such as provision and security, rather than the impacts. Yet, I crave a return to lower-stakes, shared moments of connection with my folks.

I remember a feeling of anticipation in my senior year of high school when I had been accepted into a liberal arts college in Boston and was ready to get out. I had written my personal statement about the meanings of matrilineal care, reminiscing on how my *baachan* had created a sense of cultural safety and belonging for me. In her home, I ate chicken *katsu* and *makizushi* at her kitchen table unbothered. She guided my hand with hers as she showed me how to use the wooden bamboo brush for *sumi-e*. In her home, I felt a connection to and an emerging sense of pride for family, and was able to free my mind of the confusing and self-harming thoughts about who I was supposed to be.

In my freshman fall semester at Tufts, I found myself in my first Asian American Studies course guided by my later mentor, Dr. Jean Wu, who saw a longing in me. In this intimate seminar environment, I was struck by a new line of questioning that forced me to reexamine what I thought I knew. "What are the words you need to say?" Prof. Wu asked, borrowing from Audre Lorde's writing about how our silences will not protect us. I knew then that everything I had bottled up, trying to keep down to not stick out, was meant to be released. Through dialogue with fellow queer people of color, I found a place at Tufts, and a bit more of myself. I'd like to think that against the backdrop of white, Christian, cis-hetero Boston, we chose to be in community together. What did it mean to disrupt the norms we once adhered to by simply showing up as our authentic selves? What does it mean to possess this power, this agency, *to be*? I felt as if the familial and community prescriptions of "good Japanese American" fell aside, and to be proud of the multiplicities of my being meant saying them aloud, actualizing to myself that I am here and I have something special to offer this world. I am forever grateful for the queer, femme Asian American and BIPOC mentors who I met in college. I am also proud of myself for taking the needed risks to explore and expand my sense of trust to queerness and how new relationships to each other can be formed.

I believe the COVID-19 pandemic prompted a similar investigation to the question of "who cares for me/us?" When shelter-in-place began, I had choices to make based on how the structures around me, including the guarantee of work and income, fell through. I moved down to LA ahead of a graduate school program and was forced to slow down when it seemed like the possibility of social gatherings would not happen again. I leaned on cooking, yoga, and the work of adrienne maree brown to find some center. I made it a priority to visit my *baachan* weekly, watching her age and lose her social routine as Venice Community Center classes were halted. No longer able to cook as much as she once could, I paid attention to how she held space in her kitchen and in her backyard garden. I have also been privy to her daily grievances, as the passing of her family and friends have come sharply and left her deeper in solitude. Since first writing this piece, my *baachan* has also passed on at the age of 95. Through writing, I've been able to honor her care and love for family over the entirety of her life.

In many ways, I got to know my *baachan* more over the past 3.5 years than before by understanding her day-to-day routines. While I am nostalgic for childhood road trips to LA showered by *baachan*'s cooking, I gained a sense of duty and deeper connection when my sister, uncle and I returned to her acts of care at the end of her life. Grieving, mourning, becoming, and growing all feel compounded, and it's been difficult to define which practices for self-care help pull this collision apart. I try to show up for my dad, my uncle, my mom, and sister with a softness that I tried to share with *baachan*. I remember giving *baachan* shoulder massages, holding her arthritic hands, holding onto our grown connection. These practices breathe into me a multitude of feelings—the highs and lows of the past few years, of simply making it to tomorrow. In many ways, I've grown to accept my full queer self because I've grown to accept my family for who they are, even when they are not able to display their embrace of my queerness and my values so readily. I've found self-acceptance because I haven't given up on family, on knowing my family history, and because I know from who and where I come in their complexities. Oftentimes it doesn't feel like a big aha moment, but rather small yeses towards a greater understanding of who I am. Allowing myself to nurture the small moments with family, trying not to anticipate the "what ifs."

I'm not sure what "going home" means exactly. I think I will always be bound to a past home in which I feel parented and provided for, but may not always have the tools to express my full self freely. This home, like my inner child, shows up often, especially during times of obligatory holiday gatherings. It has also been difficult to create a new "home" in different geographies where I am physically separate and more independent, yet neither there nor here. I'm scared to lose tethers to family completely, or the memories and truths of all that my grandparents faced.

I've found a sense of "home" in LA-based organizing group Vigilant Love through their Solidarity Arts Fellowship, a program that brings together many queer Japanese American and Muslim American and centers arts-based healing justice. One journaling prompt, "Who made it possible for you to be here?" reminded me Prof. Wu and her encouragement for us people of color to keep on telling our stories. I shared stories of my late grandparents' labors, my parents' efforts to secure my sister and my futures. In this space, Vigilant Love has grounded me, humbled me even, to think about collective care beyond just myself and to recognize that our generations have tried their best with what they got. Ideally, I wish for a future in which harm is minimized. In which I'm surrounded by queer folks of color, *Nikkei* folks, and family and we are all able to celebrate each other.

The process of repair and reimagining feels hopeful. It can also feel isolating at times. But I think I've found a version of myself that can indeed take this on. And not just by myself.

I do know that home feels like when my body is at rest. When it is okay to be with others vulnerably. When my chest sips in more air, breathing in the moment around me. When I look my dearest friends and made-family in the eyes and tell them who I am and what I need. When I fall over on my yoga mat, or in real life, and can chuckle at that mistake. When I share with my folks what I'm up to without fear of judgment. And, home is always with *baachan*, even though she'd criticize a change in hair color or prodded me about when I'm getting married.

WHEN I GET HOME...

Kazumi Y.

Okaeri.

A simple sentiment, one that I heard all my life. My mother would unfailingly greet me with "*okaeri*" for years, from kindergarten to grade school, to high school, and after I got my first job. No matter what time it was, there was always an "*okaeri*" waiting when I got home.

Growing up in Hawai'i in the 70s and 80s, life was idyllic and slow-paced, with days spent surfing or swimming, and getting into all the usual trouble kids get into. However, growing up in such a tight-knit mostly Asian and White community in East Honolulu, the pressure to conform was extremely intense, especially for someone discovering their sexuality and gender identity.

I always knew I was different from the others, especially

in high school where sexuality starts coming into play. High school was a time of exploring my sexuality, and I had a boyfriend, which was scandalous in the 80s. While no one said anything overtly, the whispers of "faggots" and "*māhūs*" floated around the halls of my private school.

Upon graduation, my gay and trans friends started going to the bars, starting with Hula's on Kuhio Avenue, and eventually finding our way down 4 blocks to Fusion Waikiki, which was the local transgender club with a drag show and male revue. It was at Fusion that I finally found acceptance of myself, and I knew that the trans, or more specifically "*māhū*" identity was calling to me. I met many transgender women there who adopted me into their culture, and eventually began medical transition using black market hormones from Vietnam that the girls sold under the table at the club.

This of course led to a double life—being straight-laced during the day and hanging out at the transgender club at night. That was, until my mother found my bags of wigs and female clothing, which led to, in my parent's eyes, a tragedy worthy of the Greek authors of old. It was as if my parents had lost a child, and I believe it was at this point that a rift grew between my parents, brother, and myself.

After several years of this tension, I had the opportunity to move to California with my employer at the time and took it, no matter the cost. This allowed me the freedom to express myself and live authentically, and I enjoyed many years of this freedom, calling home occasionally, and finally felt free and able to live life without a constant masquerade. This period lasted about 20 years until 2018, when my father was diagnosed with dementia and Parkinson's disease, and my mother with a rare form of salivary gland and breast cancer. My mother was well enough to recover at home with my brother, but my father was placed in a care home as he required constant care.

By this time I had already created my own "family" comprised of friends I met here in Los Angeles, the transgender community, and my husband. Having them around is truly like having a family, and we are able to support each other as many of them are also estranged from their families due to their sexual and gender identities.

I went back to visit my parents in 2019, and the first thing my mother said at the door was "*okaeri.*" I spent a week at home visiting all my old haunts and marveled at how Hawai'i had changed. We visited my father at his care home, and he looked at me and said, "Are you home? Didn't you move to California?" which stunned everyone as he barely remembered anyone any longer. I promised to come back next year to visit again, but it was the last moment that I remember with him face to face.

During the COVID pandemic, flights to Hawai'i were reduced, and there were so many barriers just to get into Hawai'i. My brother called and said that my mother was now in hospice care, and that the facility was sealed to visitors. However, I could still call my mother and we spoke weekly.

On our last phone call, she said that she felt the need to be free, and that no matter what, she still believed in me. She asked me to finally live my life, and when asked what she meant, she said "however it is to live to bring you happiness and without regrets," a reference to the gender identity I masked whenever I went home to Hawai'i.

Soon after that, both of my parents passed away suddenly, my mother in 2020, and my father in 2021. My only notice was a terse text from my brother that they had passed away. Both times, the COVID pandemic made it very difficult to get back to Hawai'i, and my brother handled all the arrangements.

I went back to Hawai'i in 2022 after the restrictions lifted, and went back to my family home, now occupied by my brother. I haven't spoken to my brother since I first left Hawai'i in 1998, and we are currently estranged to the point of no contact. I didn't go into the house, but sat outside in the car and looked at the front door, wishing that just one last time, I could see my mother standing there and hear her say,

"*Okaeri.*"

06

THE IMPERFECT PRACTICE OF PARENTING AND ALLYSHIP

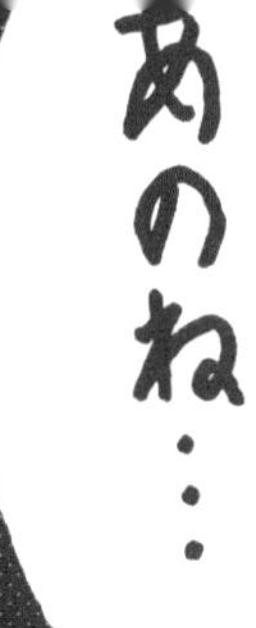

TO MY DEAREST ONE

Stacey Sagara Shigaya

You are a shining beam into humanity. You glow with confidence and love.

I never realized how much I could learn from You, could evolve, could grow—just because You are You. Unabashedly You.

I love and respect You. I am a better person because You are You. I am more patient, more understanding.

Because of You, I try hard to see The Person first—not their clothes, not their hair color, not their mannerisms. The inside of The Person—their Heart—that is the Golden Prize.

When I see people being free and confident to live their

authentic selves, I rejoice! I want to give them all a Big Hug and tell them how much I respect them and how happy I am for them.

But I can't hug everyone, so I give You extra hugs and kisses. You absorb my love from those hugs.

Let's appreciate and celebrate our Special Bond and share our love with others—whoever they may be—forever and ever.

おかえり
Hana

あなたがおなかに宿ったときから、私はあなたに夢中です。豆粒のような体の中で、小刻みに躍動するあなたの心臓を初めて見たときの感動を、今もはっきりと覚えています。毎日、あなたがお腹の中で大きくなることが奇跡のようで、いつも踊りだしたいような気持ちでした。そして、やっとあなたを腕に抱いた時、嬉しくて嬉しくて涙が自然と溢れてきました。あなたが生まれた日は、薄い雪がすべてを覆い、町じゅうに清純な空気が満ちていていました。世界のすべてがあなたの誕生を、静かに祝ってくれているようでした。

　あなたを迎えるために、壁を水色にしました。
　友人からは、恐竜やカエル、機関車トーマスのベビー服
　青や黄色や赤の色とりどりのおもちゃ

やがて、あなたが自分の好きをはっきりと伝えるようになって、家の中がディズニーのプリンセスでいっぱいになりました。プリンセスの

ティッシュボックス、絆創膏、レゴ、、、でも、私はしばらくあなたにドレスを買ってあげることができませんでした。何かそこには超えてはいけない、目に見えない一線があるような気がして、あなたの好きをちゃんと受け止めてあげられませんでした。しかし、まだ幼いあなたがドレスを前にして、私に遠慮しながら小さな声で「ほしい」とつぶやいた時、やっと目が覚めました。最初に買ってあげたドレスは、水色のスカートがフリルになったワンピースでした。初めて自分のワンピースを着たとのあなたの満面の笑顔を、今でも思い出すと胸が痛みます。なぜもっと早くあなたの願いを聞いてあげられなかったのだろう。どれほど私は、幼いあなたの心を傷つけてしまったのだろう。

それから、私の葛藤が始まりました。あなたの笑顔を守りたい。ぶしつけな質問や視線を送ってくる周りの世界から、あなたを守りたい。あなたが自由に輝くと、あなたの周りの世界の淀みが、はっきりと目に見えてくるようになりました。私は、あなたの防波堤になりたいと思いました。

あなたを守りたい。
あなたを傷つける全てのものから、あなたを守りたい。

あなたがプリスクールに行くようになって、もう私が防波堤になることができなくなりました。あなたの世界が広がったと同時に、あなたは様々な悲しみや怒りを知りましたね。ピンクの靴下をはくと、なぜ？と聞かれ、ワンピースを着たら、おかしいと言われ、ごっこ遊びで、お母さんやお姉さんになりたいとお友達にお願いしても、いつもお父さん。何度も私に悲しいと話してくれましたね。そのたびに、どうやってお友達に話しをするか、プリスクールに行く車の中でたくさん練習しましたね。あなたは、決して逃げなかった。相手を恨むこともしなかった。あなたの強さに、私はいつも驚かされ、勇気をもらっていました。そして、あなたの人生はあなたのものだと、やっと気づくことができました。あなたの代わりに、あなたの悲しみや苦しみを背負うことはできないのだと、そんな当たり前のことを認めるのが、本当はとてもつらかった。なぜなら、今まで一心同体のようにいつも一緒にいたあなたを手放すような気がして、さみしかったから。そして、あなたをすべてから守り切ることができないのだと知り、どうしようもない無力感も感じたから。

あなたは幼稚園にあがり、そして小学校へと進みました。その間も、あなたは絶えず自分であるために闘ってきましたね。幼稚園から伸ばし始めた髪の毛も、今では腰を超えました。私よりずっと長い髪の毛を、毎朝自分で上手に結って、元気に学校へ向かうあなたを、いつも誇らしく思っています。年を追うごとに、自分の力でどんどん世界を広げていくあなたを見て、私はあなたをどこまでも続く大空へと手放したのだと、あなたが帰ってくるのを楽しみに待っていられるようになりました。

これから思春期。あなたを待ち受ける現実は、つらく厳しいものでしょう。未来を想うと、弱い私の心は、すぐにでも不安でいっぱいになってしまいます。しかし、この人生はあなたのもの。あなたならきっと乗り越えて、私が想像もできなかった明るい未来へと羽ばたいていけると信じています。

私は、あなたが疲れた時に休めるよう、いつも両手を広げてあなたを待っています。あなたが悲しみの深淵にいて、そこから逃れようともがき、その刃の矛先に私が立たされたとしても、私のあなたへの愛は全く傷つきません。なぜなら、あなたの体がどんなに大きくなっても、私の目にあなたは、両手を伸ばして抱き上げられるのを待つ小さな赤ちゃんに映るのだから。

　　だから、安心して帰っておいで。

あなたが道に迷った時は、私を思い出して。ただ毎日が幸せと喜びでいっぱいだった子供のころ、私の腕の中で満ち足りた笑顔にあふれていたあの充足感。きっと大丈夫。あなたはまたこの世界に立ち向かって行ける。

私の大切な愛しいわが子。
いつもいつもあなたを想っています。
だからいつでも帰っておいで。
お母さんの腕の中に。

おかえりイラスト解説
Pepu

　トランスジェンダーの子どもにとって、カミングアウトすることは、死ぬか生きるか、というくらい深刻なことである場合が多いと思います。息子は、母親の私がアライだということは充分わかっていました。私が常日頃から、カミングアウトしてきたLGBTQの子どもを家から追い出す親がいるなんて！と嘆いていたことや、そういう子どもが、LAのような都会でホームレスになったり、生きるために売春したりしているということを嘆いていたことも知っていました。そういう我が子でさえ、悩んだ挙句にカミングアウトしてきたのです。

　ある親御さんと同席したことがあります。その人は、トランスの息子は、昔は幸せな女の子だった。あの頃の幸せな子どもに戻ってほしい、と泣いていました。認めたいけれど、小さい頃の幸せだった子どものことが忘れられず、嘆き悲しみ、そのことでお子さんからあまり話してもらえなくなった、ということも嘆いていました。

　親として、子どもがカミングアウトする前の状態を懐かしがったり、自分が

あのね…
お母さん、「わたし」じゃなく「ぼく」って言いたいんだ
お父さん、スカートもワンピースも着たくないんだ
今までずっとがまんしてきたんだ
恐くて言えないんだ
抱きしめたいわけじゃないのに
自慢の娘でいられたら…
いや…
なんでもない…

一番いいと思う状態で子どもが生きていないことをくよくよ思うこともあるでしょう。感情自体に良い悪いはないと思います。その感情をどう表すかが問題なのだと感じます。世界中が敵だと感じている我が子に対し、そういった感情を第一面に出してしまうことが、どんなに子どもを傷つけるかわかってほしいと思います。悲しんだり残念がったり怖がったりしてもいい。でも、子どもにはそれを見せない。そのくらいの親力を持ってほしい。

　親として子どもを守ってあげたいのでしょう？助けてあげたいのでしょう？それとも、子どもに気を遣わせて、自分の感情を安らかにしてもらいたいの？

　自分の子どもを受け入れられない、受け入れようとはしてるけれど、自分がつらい、そういうことを感じている親御さんに気づいてほしい。本当につらいのは誰なのか。そういう気持ちの現れがこのイラストです。トランスジェンダーの子どもにとって、世界は、敵だらけのところに思えるでしょう。せめて自分の家だけは安全で、ただいまと言って帰ってきたら安心できる場所であるべきだと思います。

幸せへの一番の近道
A SHORTCUT TO HAPPINESS

Pepu

　本人も私たちも、息子は女の子なんだと思っていました。おままごとなどの、いわゆる女の子っぽい遊びが大好きでした。13歳になってほどなく、自分はノンバイナリーだからこれからはTheyを使ってほしい、と言ってきました。その時は、私も夫も、1人なのにTheyなんて間違ってるじゃんと言って笑い、息子の心を深く傷つけてしまいました。それからほんの2〜3週間のうちに、やはり男だからこれからはHeと呼んでくれ、と言われました。息子の心の安定を図るため、私は100％協力するように努めました。

　それまでの何年間かの間、息子は、不安症に悩まされたりパニックアタックを起こしたりしていました。小さいころから我が強く、欲しいものがその瞬間に手に入らないと、大声をあげたり泣きわめいたりする子どもでした。最初はその延長だと思っていました。問題行動を起こし、中学校の校長からセラピーに連れて行くようにと言われるまでは、セラピスト探しさえしていませんでした。本人がセラピーに対して拒否反応を起こしていたこともあり、そのうち収まるだろうという楽観視もあったせいです。一旦セラピーにかかり始めてからは、ジェンダーアイデンティティーの話ばかりしていたようです。

　中学校の教師も生徒も、息子のトランジションをすんなり受け入れていました。が、女子校であったため高等部には進まず、最寄りの現地高校に、最初から男子として入学しました。その頃にはGender Dysphoriaの診断も受け、出生証明書の性別も変え、ホルモンセラピーも始め、二次性徴抑制のインプラントも入れ、胸を締め付けるバインダーもしており、見た目は男子でした。校長はLGBTQに理解の深い人だったのですが、残念ながら、生徒はマッチョカルチャーに根付いた言動を繰り返していたそうです。そのため、息子は、いつかばれるのではないか、という恐怖に怯えていました。乳房除去手術が終われば気持ちが落ち着くかと期待しましたが、そうはならず、やがて登校できなくなりました。結局、同じ学校区のオンラインハイスクールに転入することになりました。

　今息子は大学生で、クラスはハイブリッドなので、週2日は登校しています。一番落ち込んでいた時期に比べれば、随分気持ちが楽になったようです。それでも時折、不安な気持ちを口にしています。ただでさえ鬱や不安症に引き戻されそうになるというのに、LGBTQ、特にトランスジェンダーを標的にする政治家や有名人や団体が力を振るっていることを考えると、煮えたぎるような怒りを感じます。

　私にとって息子は、自分の命、夫の命、それに大切な2匹の猫の命を足しても足りないくらい重要な存在なので、最初から絶大な協力体制を敷くつもりでした。不勉強で傷つけたこともありますが、そういう時は真摯に謝りました。そして、自分の言動が息子に与えるメッセージをちゃんと自覚するようにしてきました。

　そういう自覚に至った気づきの瞬間を鮮明に覚えています。息子が中学校の卒業式に着る男児用スーツを直してあげているときでした。夜も遅くなっていました。私が直しては、息子が着て鏡の前に立ち、ここがどうのあそこがどうの、と不満を口にしていたときです。私は疲れており、息子は鏡に映る自分を見ることさえつらかったようで、不機嫌で、どこをどう直しても自分の体つきが女っぽいことを嘆いていました。何度目かに直し、やはり息子が同じようにぼやいたとき、私の平静心が崩れ、つい「じゃあこれ以上どうしろっていうの！」と声を荒げてしまいました。それと同時に、頭の中で冷静な意識があるのを感じました。「私が本当に望んでるのは何だ？」それは、息子がどんなに体型のことで悩んでいても、じっと我慢して愚痴も言わず、私に都合のいい子どもでいることか？それが私が望んでいることか？いや、違う！私にしか言えない悩みは、どんどん言ってもらわなきゃ困る。つまり、私はいつも息子の愚痴の受け皿でいなくちゃいけない。ただでさえつらい気持ちで生きている我が子に、私の感情にまで気を遣えなんて言ってる場合か？これは開眼の一瞬でした。

　私はすぐに息子に言いました。今の態度は間違ってた。ごめん。苦しくても我慢して、これでいいよ、お母さんありがとう、とか言ってほしいわけじゃないからね。これからもつらい気持ちはどんどんお母さんに言ってね、と。

　こういう学びの体験も経て、私は、息子がカミングアウトしてからずっと寄り添ってきました。夫は私のように手放しでは共感できず、苦しみながら徐々に乗り越えていく、という至極当然な反応をしていました。夫なりの全面的な協力はしていましたが、私はその間夫を反面教師として学び、ちゃっかりと高ポイントを獲得し続けていました。そのお陰で、息子は私には大抵のことは打ち明けてくれ、19歳の今でも、小さいの頃のように仲良くしてくれます。

　トランスの子を持つ他の親御さんにとって、子どもを無条件で受け入れることは、必ずしもたやすいことではない、ということは充分承知しています。私が特別だというわけではありません。私にとっては、全面的に受け入れることが一番簡単で、一番幸せに繋がりやすいやり方だったに過ぎません。ただ正直に言うと、これが、トランスジェンダーの子を持つ家族の最低レベルのあり方であるべきだという気がします。そうあってほしいと思います。

　息子が「ただいま」と帰ってきたら「おかえり」と迎える。そしてあり余るやすらぎが得られる場所として私自身が機能したい、そういう「おうち」に私自身がなりたい、と思っています。そして世界中にいるトランスジェンダーの家族も、同じような安らぎの「おうち」になってほしいと願っています。

THE GOLDEN RULE & THE SPIRIT OF OKAERI:
A LESSON FROM MY MOTHER
Jeri Okamoto-Tanaka

"You're such a fairy," I snarled at my younger brother Dave as we jostled in the family bathroom while brushing our teeth. "Am not," he cried back. "Fairy!" I shouted. "Am not!" As 9 and 11-year old siblings we constantly taunted each other, and this night in the early 1970s was no different until our mother stepped in.

"Jeri! What did you call your brother?" she demanded, her nightgowned silhouette blocking the doorway.

"A fairy," I muttered.

"Do you even know what that means?" she asked.

"Not really," I admitted, shrugging my shoulders. I had just heard the kids at school call each other that to be mean.

"Sit down, both of you." Our mother leaned against the bathroom sink as my brother and I took our places on the edge of the bathtub.

"How do you feel when someone calls you a Jap?" she asked quietly. My brother and I had endured a lot of name-calling as the only Japanese Americans, and often as the only students of color in our schools and neighborhoods. Constantly moving for our father's work, we were always the "new kids" and initiation into school—especially for my brother—included, at best, teasing and, at worst, getting beaten. Kids slanting the corners of their eyes was the universal greeting. Being called a "Jap"—being Japanese—felt scary and demeaning. I wanted to disappear or somehow transform my body into someone else who blended in, who was not Japanese. For my brother, hearing "Jap" signaled an imminent pummeling. The police delivered him home twice following school brawls. Our home—with my mother—was a safe place, our place of *okaeri* no matter where we lived or whom we encountered.

The look on my face must have betrayed my shame in how I had treated my brother. My mother's face softened. "I'm sorry, Davey," I offered, "I won't say it again." But my mother did not let it go, sensing what we would now call a teachable moment.

"What do you think it means to call someone a fairy?" she asked. Silence. I cannot remember her exact words, but that moment's anguish is stamped on my heart. She explained the different ways that people love one another and that there was nothing wrong with loving and being in love with a person of the same gender. To call someone a fairy was to make fun of or criticize who they are. It was as wrong and hurtful as being teased for being Japanese; and being Japanese or gay was not shameful.

I reflect on how affirming this exchange would have been had my brother and I been questioning our gender identity or sexual orientation at the time or later in life. I took for granted that we would be welcomed home with loving acceptance, regardless of our sexuality or whom we loved.

I wish that I could revisit this moment with my mother. How did she, a *Nisei* Japanese American woman born and raised in a small coal mining town in Wyoming during the Depression, become so wise? That we could have that talk in the early 1970s in Helena, Montana was a gift, and set the foundation for years of conversations with her about homophobia, racism, sexism, the sexual orientation of those in my dance community, the destruction of HIV/AIDS, and what she should bring to dinner with her neighbors—a gay couple who looked after her as an older woman living alone. We discussed what it meant to be transgender while watching a poignant 1975 two-part television episode of *Medical Center*, starring the dad from *The Brady Bunch* who transitioned from male to female. My family happily shared a *teppan* dinner table with drag queens after my 9th grade graduation.

I recognize that most children then and now do not have a mother so willing to initiate such discussions or to assert so clearly what love and inclusion truly mean in a diverse world. Indeed, many have parents who condemn such viewpoints and teach the opposite.

My mother died suddenly in 1992, so by the time I thought to ask about how she became such an affirming presence, it was too late. I have tried to piece together how she came to be an LGBTQ+ ally based on my own experiences as a Japanese American woman and mother, sharing that same urgency in making sure my children and their peers understand and embrace the expansiveness of gender identity and sexual orientation, and know that they have a home in this world. Given these foundational teachings from my mother and her actions, my lived experience as a *Sansei* and my allyship with the LGBTQ+ community are braided together as tightly as my girlhood ponytails.

***

My mother's life credo was simply the Golden Rule: "do unto others as you would have them do unto you," meaning treat and love others as you wish to be treated and loved. She had her own experiences of being marginalized and discriminated against as a Japanese American. She was the youngest daughter of immigrant parents. Her family lived in poverty and often depended on the kindness of Wyoming townsfolk. Yet, the local Methodist church looked beyond stereotypes, headlines, and appearances, and supported her family even during wartime when Japanese Americans from the west coast were scapegoated and incarcerated. This is how she came to the Christian faith, but her empathy and compassion were not necessarily grounded in scripture or religious doctrine, but in a belief that we ought to love and care for one another as decent human beings. I appreciate now how my mother showed "radical hospitality," even to those who teased and bullied us. She modeled the Golden Rule by welcoming my teachers and classmates to our home for a Japanese dinner (with fried chicken too). "It's harder to be mean to someone if you've eaten together in their home," she would say.

My mother's deeds matched her beliefs. At bedtime, she chanted a blessing for protection in Japanese, then reminded me—and perhaps herself—that God loves all people, including little Japanese girls; comforting words to hear, especially on days tainted with bigotry. Those were the prayers that I'm sure she said with my brother and me after the incident in the bathroom.

***

My mother's Golden Rule became the basis of my own belief system and allyship as I grew into adulthood with LGBTQ+ classmates, colleagues, extended family, and friends. But, as homophobia and anti-LGBTQ+ rhetoric and hate crimes escalated, I realized that simply proclaiming "do unto others" and providing radical hospitality did not hold up to those pointing to the Bible as the infallible authority for hate and exclusion. More was required of me as an LGBTQ+ ally, especially in social justice and faith spaces. I had to learn how to respond to the argument that "the Bible says…" with knowledge and conviction. I also had to learn how to explain how one could be both a Christian and an LGBTQ+ person or ally to my young daughters, who were confused by the hate they heard from so-called Christians. My mother's teachings gave me the belief that all are loved, but I needed back-up.

Being an LGBTQ+ ally—and a *Nikkei* ally—is not a one-and-done proclamation. To the contrary, meaningful allyship is an ongoing and humble journey. Allyship involves constantly raising my own awareness, discovering blind spots, and researching the history and intersectionality of LGBTQ+, *Nikkei*, and other generational and cultural aspects of who we have been, who we are, and who we aspire to become. This includes being accountable for the physical, emotional, and spiritual harm that faith communities and dogma have inflicted on LGBTQ+ persons and those who love them.

I found that the ability to grow in allyship is amplified by doing so in community with companions and mentors, as well as those raising challenging questions that provoke deeper study and reflection. The Okaeri gatherings—that brought together *Nikkei* LGBTQ+ persons and their families, as well as Christian pastors and Buddhist priests—demonstrated the promise of healing dialogue in safe spaces. The gatherings also provided resources for my further study that I brought back to my own faith community at the West Los Angeles United Methodist Church (West Los Angeles UMC).

As a historic Japanese American church in Southern California founded by immigrants in 1930, the West Los Angeles UMC congregation knew the sting of injustice, discrimination, and exclusion as survivors and descendants of the World War II incarceration of Japanese Americans. Just as my personal experience of being targeted as an "other" provoked my empathy, so too was this congregation's understanding and compassion stirred to action in discerning who God was calling this church to be. This history and heart-to-heart conversations with LGBTQ+ members and family in the congregation moved the church to become an official ally, a rebel Reconciling Congregation affirming all as sacred beings, specifically including LGBTQ+ persons as ordained clergy and leaders, blessing same-sex marriages, and advocating for justice, inclusion, and equality.[1]

Still seeking deeper knowledge to counter anti-LGBTQ+ religious attitudes and transform hearts and minds, I answered a call to ministry. I found the spirit of *okaeri* at the Claremont School of Theology, a progressive interfaith, ecumenical, and LGBTQ+ affirming graduate school. I studied with professors and classmates in the LGBTQ+ community and other allies, adding depth and breadth to my understanding. My courses equipped me with theological scholarship, skillful means, and the compassionate practices and conviction to interpret Biblical texts in context, and to address suffering, injustice, and trauma with care.

Being an ally is more than just finding commonality and solidarity in the fight for inclusion and social justice as *Nikkei* minorities. As an ally, I must also acknowledge that there are complexities and aspects of being LGBTQ+ that I will never completely understand. But, I continue to learn.

---

1 Although debated for more than 30 years, as of this writing, United Methodist doctrine states, in part, that "the practice of homosexuality is incompatible with Christian teaching" and includes related prohibitions regarding LGBTQ+ persons in the church. A "Reconciling Congregation" takes an official stance against this doctrine and, instead, provides an inclusive LGBTQ+ welcoming and affirming community of faith. The international Reconciling Ministries Network is comprised of more than 1,000 congregations "committed to intersectional justice across and beyond the United Methodist connection, working for full participation of all LGBTQ+ people throughout the life and leadership of the church."

***

Now that I am the age my mother was when she died, I reflect on her legacy and return to where we began decades ago, with her Golden Rule teachings to treat and love LGBTQ+ persons just as all deserve and wish to be treated. These precepts are indeed grounded in scripture to love ourselves and one another profoundly, and I am blessed to be part of a vocation where I can alleviate suffering, help individuals flourish, confront injustice, and create safe, spiritual spaces for the LGBTQ+ and ally community. And, like my mother, I teach children about expansive and inclusive love through demonstrating belonging and compassion.

By our words, deeds, and allyship, we can guide this next generation toward a more loving world that is a welcoming home to all, reflecting the generous spirit of *okaeri*. Just one compassionate and LGBTQ+ affirming conversation can recalibrate the trajectory of a life toward love and affirmation.

LISTEN
Carl Ichikawa

As a *Sansei* married to a Japan-born wife, "*okaeri*" was a daily greeting upon returning home. But as the father of two daughters who are members of the LGBTQ+ community, *okaeri* now means a welcoming to a wider group. After being introduced to Okaeri in 2020, I felt a connection to the JA community that was different from my past associations through church or cultural activities. This new connection was as a parent and ally reaching out to other parents of the LGBTQ+ community.

Our family has traveled through one daughter's transition and a second daughter's marriage to a partner of the same gender. Our youngest daughter was assigned male at birth, but danced as an *Onnagata* (female role) in *Nihon Buyo* (Japanese classical dance), participated as a two-season contestant on *RuPaul's Drag Race*, and is now an advocate as a transgender woman. Our eldest daughter was a single mom who recently married her loving partner.

The feeling of *okaeri* came to life for me when our youngest daughter was deciding whether to join our annual holiday gathering of the clan in 2018. It would be the first time since completing her transition and I had no idea she was so anxious about attending. After all, this was her extended family of aunts, uncles, and cousins who had known her since birth. And that's when she explained that it's harder to meet people who knew her before her transition as their memories are of a different person. Would people be accepting of her? Would they misgender her? Would they act differently? I decided to share with the family that our daughter would be attending and asked for their understanding as it would be her first holiday with her new identity. The responses were an unexpected "we already know." Whew, I was relieved and our daughter decided to come home. That day, she was nervous but as the family started to arrive, there was no hesitation, no awkward questions, though yes, an occasional misgender. Her tension and fear eased and it was a pretty normal holiday. *Okaeri* was the perfect expression of the collective love and acceptance shown that day.

Every family's journey is unique. As a parent, our youngest daughter's transition had a certain naturalness to it as we were used to seeing her present herself as a woman. Yet, I still cannot imagine the hurt, loneliness, and dangers that she had to endure and continues to face. I'm amazed at her courage and determination, but there is real joy in seeing your child live their authentic life.

For my eldest daughter who had prior boyfriends, I was surprised when she shared that her new partner was a woman. However, that momentary surprise was soon replaced with joy after we met and got to know each other. Once again, seeing your child happy and living their life is so satisfying for any parent.

I realize that not all families are as fortunate as ours. Fortunate as in no outright rejection or hostility. Fortunate as in being supportive and trying to use the correct pronouns. Fortunate as in being able to express what we are feeling.

But, we are also far from conflict-free. We disagree, we argue, we get mad, we make mistakes. Even so, I can honestly say that I feel closer to my daughters today than I did before, as we talk more now even though we live 2,000 miles apart.

One thing I've had to learn is to be an active listener. As a father, I saw my role as the fixer, someone who was expected to have the answers. While I'm never shy to share my opinion, sometimes the best thing we can do is to be quiet and listen. Listen to the hurt, the joy, the confusion, and the triumphs that our adult children want to share with us. It not only gives me a better understanding of their lives, but makes me appreciate that they even want to share their stories with me.

For those who are members of any religious group, such groups can be either a source of support or conflict. At my local Buddhist temple, the welcoming message at the doorway entry is "Come as you are" which I have always been grateful to see. The temple has been an important part of my life, and has also been a source of education where I've learned of initiatives such as the Ichi-Mi project, which looks to help educate temples and organizations on improving LGBTQ+ inclusivity. However, one of my hopes going forward is to have the courage to be a more visible ally. A key event for me was when my daughter and I were interviewed for the temple newsletter. This was my "coming out" to our members as the father of an LGBTQ+ child. A few members made supportive comments, which I hoped was the majority view. I think those of us from the Japanese American community have been conditioned to see silence as agreement, or at least acceptance. It is only recently that I've learned from others that even if this is true, silent acceptance may not be enough.

Especially in these difficult times, allies should consider stepping beyond our comfort zone to speak up. For me, that means sharing my experiences as the father of two LGBTQ+ daughters, with the hope that another person hearing my story may realize they are not alone, and that there are many in the same situation. We are your neighbors, your coworkers, your family. Listening to others helps remove the isolation that can be a heavy burden to carry, and in turn, your story becomes the stepping stone for the next person to take that first step forward in their understanding of who they or their family members truly are. I still remember my first step was joining my company's Pride group and displaying a Pride pin in my cubicle. It was a small but important step for me.

As a parent, our goal is to nurture our children to be independent adults. And yet, when their dreams don't align with ours, there may be disappointment or disapproval. For families within the community, matters of personal identity can cause anger, confusion, perhaps even estrangement. But as a parent, put aside your fears and stand by your child. Support them, listen to them, love them. They need you even if they don't say it directly. By coming together as a caring family, we can celebrate our differences while being unwavering in our love and support for one another.

THE EVOLUTIONARY JOURNEY OF MOTHERING

Judy Yushin Nakatomi

First published in Lions Roar, 2022

On the evolutionary journey of mothering, I'm practicing imperfectly. As the proud mother of two adult daughters, ages 31 and 27, who are multi-ethnic, transfemme, and queer, my journey of motherhood has not been a linear one. Both of my children came out separately in their twenties, which didn't take me by complete surprise. Since they were young, I've had an inner knowing that they were each on their own journey, and that their paths could take many directions.

Looking back, their interests and choices were more fluid than fixed by any set of "rules" presented to them, which wasn't always met with approval and acceptance from the adults in their lives. Both of my children didn't align with traditional gender norms or rules in school that governed their social behavior or choice of activities, hobbies, or friends. As they grew into adulthood, I became more curious and excited to see who they were becoming. It felt like I was being invited to witness budding flowers bloom. An inner voice whispered: Wait patiently, keep caring and tending.

> *In its most exquisite sense, to mother is about caring*
> *for the well-being of another being; it's about loving,*
> *kindness, empathy, protection, and having a long*
> *view of being and time.*

Throughout their growing up, my daughters have continually taught me how to expand and deepen my awareness of what it means to love in more boundless and spacious ways. There have been times when I've mothered unskillfully. Early on, I misgendered our eldest daughter (who uses they/she pronouns) without realizing the full impact of my actions. It was then that I began to observe more closely and listen more deeply.

As a Japanese American, I know how racial microaggressions impact my own body. I began to see how my actions of not fully "getting it" impacted and hurt my children. I recognized that I could be more vocal when I witnessed misgendering happening with family and friends. As a cisgender, heterosexual woman, I could make clear and direct corrections to family and friends while educating them about my own journey of learning to recognize and correct my mistakes.

At times, I let my fear for my childrens' safety overshadow

their need to live a full life. I was aware that trans and queer people of color experience high levels of hostility, hate, and violence. I was also aware that leading with the vibration of fear created the rigid, tight energy that I longed to transform. I needed to remind myself that embodying joy and delight creates very strong vibrations, too. Artistic expression, through dance and music, are a vital part of both my daughters' lives—I wished to nourish and water the joy of their art. As I educate myself and meet more LGBTQ+ parents, fear is no longer front and center. This has all been a part of the journey to unfurl and flow with the joy and vibrancy in their lives.

Our loving actions can play a vital role in transforming homophobia and transphobia. I use my voice and writing to share how I'm awakening. I point to the ways I've been unskillful with a promise to keep learning and growing, because to mother is to have the energy of empathy and the spirit to nurture and protect, which for me is closely connected to the Primal Vow in Shin Buddhism.

The Primal Vow is the 18th verse of the *Larger Sukhavativyuha Sutra*, or *Infinite Life Sutra*, which describes the *bodhisattva* vow of manifesting boundless compassion and liberation for all beings in everyday life, where all are worthy, all belong, and no one is forgotten, abandoned, or neglected. Part of the practice is *gassho* (palms together), and reciting the *nembutusu: Namu Amida Butsu.* To me, mothering exemplifies how I interpret the Vow to continue to show up to transform homophobia and transphobia through the actions I take in daily life; to be the sister, friend, and mother who steps up to point to a way through fear and harmful views, speech and actions. Along my daughters' journeys, it became clear to me that I needed to show up for them in my everyday life with my family and friends too. In speaking to some friends and family, I sensed there might be tension or misunderstanding about my children's gender or expression. I began to frame the narrative, "I know you have loved our kids from the day they were born" to declare that as my continued hope and expectation. I affirmed their love while offering advice on ways they could show up more: honoring pronouns, educating themselves, asking questions, checking in directly with my daughters, and offering educational resources.

I began to be an advocate and a bridge to help our family and friends understand how to best show their love and acceptance for our daughters' gender identities and sexual orientation. I worked to openly answer their questions and am still learning ways to be an ally to my children and the LGBTQ+ community through groups like PFLAG and Okaeri. In *Shin* and *Zen sangha* spaces, I also make sure to share my pronouns and explain why it's important.

Today, I have a different view of mothering. I recognize that "mothering" isn't limited to biological, adoptive, step, or foster mothers. To me, mothering in its most expansive sense is not defined by gender identity—to care in the fullest sense includes all, leaving out no one, no body.

Mothering adult transfemme and queer children is an ever evolving and fluid practice. If I consider the word "mother" as a verb, "mother" is queer. How can we compartmentalize or restrict care, love, and empathy to a binary? In its most exquisite sense, to mother is about caring for the well-being of another being; it's about loving, kindness, empathy, protection, and having a long view of being and time.

The Three Doors of Liberation[1] also help me cultivate awareness around the transient nature of notions, form, and goals, and remind me to ultimately let go.

Through this viewpoint of impermanence, I continue to practice imperfectly on the path of mothering. This ride flows, unfurls, and opens in a non-linear way. Mothering is a continuum—an evolutionary ride of caring, learning, and protecting.

---

1 The first door—emptiness—reminds us that we are connected to all sentient beings; there is no separation or exception. The second door—signlessness—recognizes that form is continually changing and signs can be deceiving. Our thoughts, words and actions are of the nature to change too, so we build awareness around our attachments. For example, a cloud does not cease to exist when it becomes rain, mist, fog, or snow. A cloud continues in another form. The third door—aimlessness—is where we release our tight grip on a goal or destination, and become more aware that dualistic thinking can cause much suffering (i.e. negative/positive, either/or, coming/going).

OUR STORY IN TRANSLATION

Stacia Kato

English	Japanese
Japanese is my second language. Please forgive my mistakes in grammar and lack of vocabulary.	日本語は私の第二言語です。文法や言葉の間違いを大目に見てください。

Allow me to start my story from today. I am the proud mother of a 21-year-old transgender daughter named Alex. That means she was assigned male at birth and she came out to me at 16 as a transgender woman. We refer to her with she/her pronouns because she is trans feminine. Her original name was "Alexander Toshizo Kato" and we still use her shortened name, "Alex," because women can also have the name "Alex."	現在の状況から話を始めさせてください。私はアレックスという19歳の娘を誇りに思う母親です。娘はトランスジェンダー、つまり出生時に男性に割り当てられました。娘は１６歳のときにトランスジェンダー女性として私に「カミングアウト」しました。彼女は女性なので、私たちは「彼女」という女性の代名詞を使っています。「アレックス」は女性の名前でもあるため、私たちは娘をまだアレックスと呼んでいます。
Today she has good friends, she drives and maintains her car, cooks our meals (because my husband and I work from home), she attends community college full-time, and is learning to become a CNC machinist to build precision metal parts.	彼女は彼女には良い友達がいて、愛車のメンテと運転もし、夫と私は自宅で仕事をしているため、家族の食事も作ってくれます。精密金属部品を作るためのCNC機械工になるの目標の為フルタイムで短大に通っています。

Most importantly, she is happy, healthy, and learning to make a good living. I imagine that is what parents all want for our children, yes?	今、娘は幸せで健康で良い生活を送ることを学んでいます。それは皆、親として我が子に望んでいることだと思いませんか。
Those who know me, know that I am a strong advocate for Asian Pacific Islanders and LGBTQ+ people. I spend much of my free time to share our story and help educate others about parenting a transgender child because I have already walked this journey.	私を知っている方は、私がアジア系達とLGBTQ+の人達の為に熱心に活動していることを知っています。私はすでにこの旅路を歩んで来たものとして、トランスジェンダーの子供を育てる事について他の人のお役に立てる様、時間が許す限り我が家の話をシェアしています。
Let me tell you first, I am not a perfect parent. I am very far from being a perfect parent. And that is OK. I like to think that I am learning and growing as a person along with my child. In fact, there are so many things I learned from my child over the years.	最初に申し上げますが、私は完璧な親ではありません。完璧な親からほど遠いです。それでも大丈夫。私は子供と一緒に人として学び成長していると思うのが好きです。実際、何年にもわたって子供から学んだことはたくさんあります。

The idea that we, as parents who are older and have more experience, could learn from our children may not feel comfortable. However, I feel the world is changing and our young people have so much to teach us, if we are open to learning it.	私たちが年長で経験豊富な親として子供たちから学ぶことができるという考えは、しっくりこないかもしれません。しかし、世界は変化しています。私たちが学ぶ事に前向きであるなら、若者は私たちに教えることが沢山あると感じています。
I learned that Alex's brain is different. When my child was in middle school, she struggled. Alex is a naturally bright child, but the structure of school did not align with how her brain works. She was diagnosed with ADHD, but I didn't pay attention to this because she was still able to get good grades.	アレックスは中学生の時、苦労しました。学校構成が彼女の思考と合っていなかったのです。彼女は生まれつき頭の良い子供ですが、私は彼女の脳のはたらきが他の人と違うことを知りました。彼女はADHDと診断されたのですが、まだ良い成績を取得することができたので、私はこれに注意を払いませんでした。

When she got to high school, she told me to sit down because she had something important to tell me. She said she was afraid she would commit suicide because she was so depressed.	高校に入学したとき、彼女は「話したい大切なことがある」と、私を座らせました。娘は、「とても落ち込んでいる自分が自殺するのではないかと不安だ」と言ったのです。
At this point, she had not come out yet. I did not know what was wrong. I thought, maybe it is because her father and I are divorced. Maybe I work too hard and I do not pay enough attention to her. Why was my child suffering so much?	当時、彼女はまだカミングアウトしていませんでした。私には何が原因なのかわかりませんでした。彼女の父親と私が離婚したのが原因？もしかして私は仕事に夢中になり過ぎて、娘に注意を払っていなかったのだろうか。なぜ私の子供はそんなに苦しんでいるのだろうか？。
I took her to a therapist. A male therapist. I thought maybe she was sad because her father and I are divorced and he moved back to Japan several years ago. Why was my child suffering so much?	彼女をカウンセラーに連れて行きました。男性のカウンセラーでした。娘は父が私と離婚して、数年前に日本に帰国したので悲しいのではないかと思ったからです。なぜ私の子供はそんなに苦しんでいたのだろうか？

After two years of therapy with two different therapists, allowing Alex to leave high school to start college early, and the use of antidepressant medication, Alex sat me down again. This time, to tell me she is a transgender woman. She was afraid to tell me, but also afraid not to tell me about such an important part of her life.	それから2年間、アレックスは二人のカウンセラーからカウンセリングを受けました。やがて娘は高校を卒業し大学を始め、抗うつ剤も使い始めまた。そんな時、アレックスは再び私を座らせました。今度は、自分がトランス女性だと言う為に。伝える事を恐れてた一方、彼女の人生で大事なことを私に伝えていない恐れもあったそうです。
My first reaction was "...but I know you like women..." but I quickly realized a person's gender is not the same as a person's sexuality. Who you are inside is a different matter than who you are attracted to outside.	私の最初の反応は…「でもあなたは女性が好きでしょう…」でした。でも、性別は性的指向と同じではないことにすぐ気づきました。自分が内面誰であるかと自分が外面どんな人に惹かれるからは別である。

I could see the hope on Alex's face, the hope that I would understand her, not be angry, and not reject her. And I looked at her and said, "I just want you to be happy, healthy, learn how to make money, and take care of me when I'm an old lady." She agreed and we hugged.	そのとき私はアレックスの表情に希望が溢れるのを目の当たりしました。私が彼女を理解し、怒つり彼女を拒絶したりしないという希望です。そこで私は彼女に向き合って、「あなたには幸せで健康で、お金を稼げる様になり、私がおばあさんになったら世話してもらう事だけ望んでるよ」と言いました。彼女は同意し私達はハグしました。
I learned that there is nothing I or her father did wrong. Nothing we did as parents "caused" her to be this way. She is who she is. I also learned that accepting her as a girl was very important for her mental health.	私も彼女の父親も、間違ったことは何もしていなかったと気づきました。両親としてした事で彼女が「こうなった」原因ではありませんでした。彼女はそれがありのままの彼女なのです。そして彼女を女性して受け入れることは、彼女のメンタルヘルスにとって非常に重要であることも学びました。

I had already seen her through two years of anxiety and depression. Some days, she could not go to school. In fact, the psychologist told me to lock up any sharp objects in the house so that Alex would not use it to harm herself.	私はすでに2年もの間、不安と鬱病に悩む娘を見てきました。通学出来ない日もありました。アレックスが自分自身を傷つけないよう家中の刃物になるものを閉まって鍵をかける様心理学者が私に勧めたこともありました。
So when Alex "came out" to me, it was a relief to know something so important about her that I could learn more about. I learned as much as I could in English through many resources like Okaeri, PFLAG, Transforming Family, even Facebook groups. The more that I learned, the more comfortably I could interact with my child.	アレックスが私に「カミングアウト」した時、娘についてとても重要な事をもっと学ぶことができると知って安心しました。Okaeri, PFLAG, Transforming Familyなど沢山の英語リソースを通じて、出来る限り多く学びました。Facebookグループにまでも参加しました。学べば学ぶほど、子供とよりスムーズに交流することができるようになりました。

I realized I had to share this information with my husband, who is Alex's stepfather. Thankfully he understood enough to support me as Alex's primary parent. Even if he didn't understand what it means to be transgender, he knew not to make me choose between him and my child.	私は、アレックスの継父にあたる今の夫にもこの情報を共有しなければいけないと気づきました。ありがたいことに、彼はアレックスの親である私をサポートすることが大切だと十分理解していました。トランスジェンダーであることが何を意味するのか理解していなくても、夫は彼か我が子を選ぶような選択を私に迫りませんでした。
Then, I learned, I needed to understand how to explain this to her biological father, my ex-husband, who is a Japanese native and living in Japan. I found more resources in Japanese in the World Professional Association for Trangender Health (WPATH) Standards of Care. And, her father was able to attend some Japanese sessions with Okaeri in 2018 when we came out to him.	それから、娘の実の父親である元夫に彼女がトランスジェンダーであることを日本生まれの日本在住である元夫に説明して分かってもらえるには、工夫が必要だと悟りました。日本語のリソースが World Professional Association for Trangender Health (WPATH) Standards of Care を通してもっと見つかりました（リソースリストを共有します）。実際、彼女の父親は、私たちが彼にカミングアウトした2018年、オカエリコンファレンスでいくつかの日本語セッションに参加する事ができました。

That was five years ago. Alex has been taking hormone replacement medicines for over two years. Her body has changed. More importantly, her heart and mind have become more peaceful. I have learned so much and I share very publicly, but I do not expect Alex to share. For me, as a parent, it is my responsibility to make the world a safer place for my child. And that is why I share our story.

Thank you for listening.

あれから３年が過ぎました。アレックスは2年以上ホルモン剤を服用しています。彼女の体は変わりました。さらに、彼女の心はより落ち着きました。私は沢山のことを学びました。そして、私は自分の体験をとてもオープンにシェアしています。でもアレックスがシェアすることを期待しません。私の子供にとって世界をより安全な場所にすることは親である私の責任です。だから、私は私とアレックスの体験を皆さんにお伝えするのです。

お聞き頂き有難うございました。

CROSSED UP IN TRANSLATION

Bill Watanabe

The conservative Christian church is often seen as anti-gay. Yet in the long history of Christianity, this was not always the case.

For Christians, the Bible is considered "the word of God" so what it says about various topics is taken seriously by believers. I attended a Japanese American Christian church growing up and converted to Christianity in 1959 when I was 14 years old. In my desire to be a faithful Christian, I have embarked on a practice to regularly read and study the Bible. I love reading the Bible because its colorful stories and teachings are full of rich human experience and wisdom that can apply to my life and give me guidance. However, I would not consider myself a "Bible expert" or an informed theologian, but rather just a person trying to be faithful to the Christian life based on the teachings of the Bible.

Ten years ago, if someone had asked me whether homosexuality was a "sin," I would have answered that the Bible is pretty clear that it was indeed a sin. It says so in plain English, in at least two Biblical references, that homosexuality is sinful behavior. There are many different English translations of the Bible, and the version I have used extensively since my college days is *The New American Standard Bible* (NASB) which was originally published in 1960 and was considered by many theologians at the time as the most accurate translation of the ancient Hebrew, Greek, and Aramaic texts of the Bible. The two Bible passages to which I refer regarding homosexuals are:

- I Corinthians 6:9-10[1], which lists a group of unrighteous people who will not inherit the kingdom of God, such as: fornicators, idolaters, adulterers, nor the effeminate, homosexuals, thieves, nor the covetous, drunkards, revilers, or swindlers.
- I Timothy 1:9-10[2], which is another list of lawless and ungodly sinners such as: murderers, immoral men and homosexuals, kidnappers, liars, perjurers, and anyone opposed to sound teaching.

Because of my faith in the Bible, and the fact that homosexuals are clearly defined as sinners in these verses, I would have acknowledged this as a tenet of my Christian

---

[1] "Or do you not know that the unrighteous will not inherit the kingdom of God? Do not be deceived; neither fornicators, nor idolators, nor adulterers, nor effeminate, nor homosexuals, nor thieves, nor the covetous, nor drunkards, nor revilers, nor swindlers, will inherit the kingdom of God."

[2] "realizing the fact that law is not made for a righteous person, but for those who are lawless and rebellious, for the ungodly and sinners, for the unholy and profane, for those who kill their fathers or mothers, for murderers and immoral men and homosexuals and kidnappers and liars and perjurers, and whatever else is contrary to sound teaching..."

faith. Lately however, there have been some modifications by Christians to this tenet—stated in simple terms as "hate the sin but love the sinner," meaning that Christians can or should love and accept gay people but not endorse the gay lifestyle. I believe this modification came about when it became clear that being gay was not a choice and could not be overcome even through counseling and fervent prayer.

I have come to the realization that my views on homosexuality may have been misguided, not only for me but for all English-speaking Christians in the world. It has come to light that the Christian concept that homosexuality is a sin may be in error. In my mind, it is no longer black and white, and is theologically disputed.

About 7 years ago, I attended a seminar at Evergreen Baptist Church of Los Angeles, given by a woman named Kathy Baldock, who has been on a journey of discovery regarding how and when the word "homosexual" first appeared in the English Bible. Baldock and her colleague Ed Oxford had discovered that the word first appeared in the 1946 translation of what was called the *Revised Standard Version* of the Bible (RSV). The RSV quickly became one of the most popular versions of the English Bible, and also the foundational work upon which other English translations and spin-offs were based. Unfortunately, because the RSV contained the word "homosexual" in I Corinthians and I Timothy, many subsequent versions simply repeated the translation, which was then printed and re-printed in hundreds of millions of English Bibles.

The original text languages of the Bible are ancient

Hebrew, Greek, and Aramaic, and English translators have been attempting for centuries to accurately translate those early texts to know what the Bible actually says and means. The version that was the most popular for many generations was the *King James Bible* printed in 1611, which remained the standard until the 20th century. Many of the passages from the *King James Bible* have also become a part of our popular lexicon. In the 20th century, newer translations were printed (like the RSV and the NASB) to make the English more vernacular.

Baldock explained that the term "homosexual" did not even exist until the mid-to-late 1800s (first coined in German) and was not popularly used in American society, except perhaps amongst psychiatric professional circles. Up until 1946, the term "homosexual" did not appear in any of the earlier versions of the English Bible. In 1946, a team of theologians and language experts met at Yale University with the goal of re-writing the Bible in modern English. It is here that the term "homosexual" makes its first appearance in the Bible in I Corinthians and I Timothy.

To explain a little further about the Biblical references in question, there are a number of verses in the Bible regarding same-sex relations, though not many. In the two passages cited, the term "homosexual" appears in the RSV as a translation of the Greek words "*malakoi arsenokoitai.*" According to Christian ethicist David Gushee in his book *Changing Our Mind*, these two words are extremely difficult to translate because their usage by the biblical author 2,000 years ago is very unclear in terms of its intended meaning.

For example, some early English translations of these passages used terms such as "buggerers," "sodomites," and "self-abusers." These terms could imply illicit sex acts (at least for that period in time) but not necessarily "homosexual" activity.

The word "*malakoi*" in ancient Greek is generally translated to mean "soft" and is often used to describe something like a "soft fabric." When applied to human behavior, it could allude to a man being effeminate or to a person living a luxurious lifestyle. Some Biblical scholars feel the term could be applied to describe a male being penetrated by another male, such as in the case of male prostitution or forced sex. However, these are not clear examples of what we would consider today to be LGBTQ+ relationships.

The second Greek term "*arsenokoitai*" is extremely difficult to translate, according to Gushee, because it is such a rarely used term in ancient Greek texts outside of the Bible. It is almost impossible to cross-reference a meaning or usage of the term with other Greek writers of that period. The literal translation of the word (which is a composite of two terms) would be "man-bed." And what on earth can one clearly infer from that term?

When the two words, "*malakoi arsenokoitai*" are put together as they appear in the ancient Greek texts of I Corinthians and I Timothy, it is not possible to say with great confidence what the term actually means and what the Biblical author was trying to say. David Gushee states that a number of Biblical experts now feel that the best English translation of the terms might be along the lines of "sexual perversion" or "sexual exploitation."

This is important because if the Bible had been translated to call "sexual perversion" or "sexual exploitation" a sin instead of "homosexuality," the conservative Christian animosity towards the LGBTQ+ community might have been totally muted.

In 2017, Baldock and Oxford visited the archives at Yale University to study the actual notes left behind by the 1946 RSV translation team. To their amazement, they discovered a series of letters where the chair of the translation team admitted that they had made an error in using the term "homosexual" in their English translation of the Bible! To correct this error, the translation team replaced the word "homosexual" with the term "sexual perverts" in later reprints of the RSV, but unfortunately, it was too late to keep other Bible translations from using the incorrect RSV as their foundational text. Even today, many English Bibles still employ the term "homosexual" in their English translations, continuing the enmity perpetrated against the LGBTQ+ community.

Today, if someone were to ask me if the Bible considers homosexuality a sin, my answer would be different; I would answer "maybe, and maybe not." I would explain that the Bible is not clear on the subject, though many Christians believe it to be. I would say that there are a number of different interpretations based on translations of the Biblical texts, and a clear translation of meaning is not easily made on this issue.

It is my hope that more Christians will come to

understand that the interpretation of the Bible and the linking of the word "homosexuality" as a sin was a grievous error of translation (and perhaps bias), and that the Bible and Christian beliefs will, in the future, no longer engender animosity towards the LGBTQ+ community.

Attitudes can change. Once, people looked upon Japanese Americans only with suspicion and distrust. Anti-semitism was much more wide-spread and rampant in the past than now. Biblical perspectives about the status of women have evolved and improved. If these viewpoints can change, there is also hope for positive change for our friends in the LGBTQ+ community.

MEETINGS AT THE SHORE

Jill Togawa

The Pacific Ocean separated me from my island home for decades. Sometimes, when I missed it too intensely, I wished I could swim home. And while I chose to stay on the other shore, I never stopped yearning for simple things with my mom. An impromptu dinner or drop in visit, a movie, admiring a flower in bloom—were all luxuries that remained out of reach.

I finally live near my mother again, and ten years later I am still steeping in her sageness and care; small everyday acts of love expressed through the newspaper she saves for me, savoring pirie mangoes together, her refusal to leave a store without a small treat for my child. Attending to the evolving ways she needs me—as I once needed her—is the loftiest privilege.

Last month, we sat across the glass table from each

other on her *lanai* and lunched on her favorite beet *poke* with butternut squash *dal* and rice. So far away in my mind now, almost as though belonging to a different young person, was our brief talk in her living room on the evening more than 40 years ago when I was home from New York and so anxious to share my new understanding of myself. My straight roommate had told me another dancer I admired was lesbian, and with that small comment, unknowingly handed me the first blossom of a lei I began stringing, made of all my childhood crushes, years of feeling drawn to women, and desires I had not had a name for. When it was complete it was fragrant with awakening and I wanted to wear it everywhere, and of course show it to my mother .

Before I flew to her that unforgettable evening, I had already walked the streets of Greenwich Village discovering the gay bookstore with books by other lesbians whose stories I craved, and entered a lesbian bar for the first time, knowing it as a kind of homecoming though I was the only Asian woman in the place. I felt full of promise of all that was yet to come for me. My mother had told me I could be and do anything I wanted, and now I truly felt there would be space for me anywhere I wanted to go. I remember my surprise then when my ever-supportive mom did not admire my lei or share my exhilaration, quietly stating she "would need some time." "What do you need time for??" wondered my youthful, impatient self. But although my mom is *Sansei* and I could speak more directly with her than with my *Nisei* father, as a respectful child, I tried to swallow my disappointment.

Now, more than forty years later, I was coming out to

her again, this time for her youngest grandchild. My voice softened as I told her how much I did not want my child to hurt. On that summer day she did not look down. I gazed at her as she collected her resolve, and it was as if she outstretched her arms, offering the protection and acceptance I had wanted from her so long ago. These moments become one—the warm refuge my mother is for my transgender child is my refuge too. My child has a grandma who sees and embraces them with a fierce, wise love. I have a cherished photograph of them as they walk away from me, together. My child, at 16, is strong enough now to support their grandma if she falters. When they go for their daily walk they tell each other about their day. Grandma mostly listens and grandchild is the lookout for bumps and unexpected outside danger. They know they are there for each other.

When I sat in my own home, on the red sofa inherited from my Dad, and my child came out to my wife and I as trans, in a single moment I felt myself standing on that shore where I could greet my mother and my child in myself. As children we want and ask and want more for ourselves. But as parents our hearts sprout endless tendrils of generosity and we want and ask mostly for our children. Surprisingly, a peace, resonant and deep, is present since I came out to my mother again.

Mom, *okagesamade.*

GLOSSARY

A

Ainu - People indigenous to northern Japan/Hokkaido.

Asian American - A pan-ethnic social and political identity term referring to immigrants from Asia and their descendants in America coined by Yuji Ichioka and Emma Gee in 1968 as a direct result of cross-racial and ethnic solidarity building in the 1960s.

Aswang - An umbrella term for evil beings and creatures in Filipino folklore, including vampires, ghouls, witches, viscera suckers, and shape-shifting human-beast hybrids.

B

Baachan/Obaachan - Japanese for "grandmother."

Bingata - Traditional stenciled resist dyeing technique originating in Okinawa.

Brujas - Spanish for "witches."

C

Cisgender Heterosexual (Cishet) - A term referring to a person who is cisgender (identifies with their gender assigned at birth) and heterosexual.

Cultural Assimilation - The process where a minority group or culture comes to resemble a society's majority group by adopting their beliefs, languages, and culture.

F

Furry - A subculture characterized by its interest in anthropomorphic animal characters.

G

Gender Nonconforming - An umbrella term for those who do not follow conventional gender stereotypes, or who expand ideas of gender expression or gender identity.

H

Heteronormativity - The world view that promotes heterosexuality as the normal or ideal sexual orientation.

Homophobia - Prejudice, fear, dislike, or discrimination against the gay community and/or individuals.

I

Issei - A term meaning "first generation" which refers to Japanese immigrants who are the "first" generation in another country.

J

JACL - "Japanese American Citizens League." The JACL is a national organization whose mission is to secure and safeguard the civil and human rights of Japanese Americans and AAPI people.

M

Māhū - A Hawaiian term meaning "in the middle." Has been used in various contexts to refer to those who embody both male and female characteristics, are "third gender," or are transgender or transsexual. Was also used as a transphobic slur in the 80s but has since been reclaimed.

Misogi - A Japanese Shinto tradition involving the ceremonial purification of the whole body through washing.

MMORPG - "Massively Multiplayer Online Role-Playing Game."

N

Nikkei - A term referring to Japanese immigrants and their descendants living outside of Japan.

Nisei - A term meaning "second generation" which, in the American context, refers specifically to the American-born children of Issei immigrants.

Non-Binary - Refers to people who do not identify or subscribe to the traditional man-woman gender binary.

O

Oakland SOL - "Sustaining Ourselves Locally." SOL is a Queer and Trans People of Color housing collective.

Obento/Bento - Japanese term referring to a homemade/pre-packaged meal.

Obon Odori - A style of dance performed communally during the Japanese Buddhist festival of Obon.

Okaeri - Japanese for "welcome back" or "welcome home."

Okagesamade - A Japanese expression of gratitude that roughly translates to "It's all thanks to you."

P

PFLAG - The first and largest organization dedicated to supporting, educating, and advocating for LGBTQ+ people and their families. Formerly known as "Parents, Family, and Friends of Lesbians And Gays."

POV - "Point of View."

Q

QTBIPOC - "Queer, Trans, Black, Indigenous, People of Color."

Queer - An umbrella term typically used to refer to LGBTQ+ individuals. Though previously used as a slur, the term has been reclaimed by many parts of the LGBTQ+ movement.

R

Ryukyuan - People indigenous to the Ryukyu Islands.

S

Sangha - Generally referring to a Buddhist monastic order or community; the Community element of the Three Treasures of Buddhism, which also includes the Buddha and the Dharma.

Sansei - A term meaning "third generation" referring to the children of Nisei parents.

Sentō - A Japanese communal bath house that customers pay to enter.

Shinto - Japan's native religion which generally incorporates elements such as worship of ancestors, natural spirits, and belief in a divine or sacred power.

SRO - Single-room occupancy

Sumi-e - Traditional Japanese ink painting style.

Surippa - Japanese for "house slipper."

T

Tadaima - Japanese for "I'm home."

Tashme - One of the eight internment camps in British Columbia created by the Canadian Government during World War II to detain Japanese Canadians.

Tatami - Traditional Japanese straw flooring.

Techno-Orient - An idea examining how Asia and Asians are portrayed with hypo- or hyper-technological attributes in literary, cinematic, and new media contexts.

Transfemme - People who are assigned male at birth whose gender expression aligns more with femininity.

Transgender - A term describing a person's gender identity that does not necessarily match their assigned sex at birth.

Turtle Island - A name for Earth or North America used by some Indigenous peoples and Indigenous rights activists.

U

Uchinanchu - An ethnic group consisting of Okinawan immigrants and their descendants living in Hawai'i.

V

Vtubers - A term meaning "virtual Youtuber" which refers to an online entertainer who uses a virtual avatar generated using computer graphics.

Y

Yakuza - Japanese term generally meaning "gangster" and referring to members of organized crime syndicates in Japan.

Yonsei - A term meaning "fourth generation" referring to the children of Sansei parents.

AUTHOR & EDITORIAL TEAM BIOGRAPHIES

Aiden Takeo Aizumi (he/him) is a transman, storyteller, and activist for the LGBTQ+ community. He is currently a Athletic Director for Opportunities for Learning Public Charter Schools. Aiden graduated from the University of La Verne with a Masters in Education and was recognized as one of the "125 Most Influential" people in the 125-year history of the university. He currently serves as President of PFLAG Pasadena where he facilitates the youth group and has shared his story at high schools, colleges, churches, and corporations around the country. In his free time, Aiden enjoys playing music, traveling, photography, and spending time with his wife, Mary, and his dog Kuma.

Marsha Aizumi - I am the mother of a transgender son who started me on the path to advocate for the *Nikkei* LGBTQ+ communities and helped me find a voice I didn't know I had. Aiden and I have written a book, *Two Spirits, One Heart: A Mother, Her Transgender Son, Their Journey to Acceptance and Love*, which is in its second edition. We have travelled all over the United States to speak and I have been privileged to speak in Asia. I am the founder of Okaeri: A Nikkei LGBTQ+ Community and co-founder of PFLAG San Gabriel Valley API. I have also served on the PFLAG National Board of Directors and still serve on PFLAG National's Alumni Council. My greatest joy is to see LGBTQ+ individuals living as their true selves and their families embracing and proudly celebrating all of who they are.

Eric Arimoto, 58, is a 4th generation Japanese American gay man who grew up in the Crenshaw District of Los Angeles. Eric has served on Okaeri's Steering Committee since 2014 and is particularly interested in creating a welcoming space for *Nikkei* LGBTQ folk 40+ who—for various reasons—may feel hesitant to return to the village. Eric currently lives in Long Beach, CA with his partner Paul and is a marriage and family therapist specializing in working with LGBTQ individuals, couples, and adolescents.

Mia Barnett (she/her) is a freelance video editor and organizer based in Los Angeles with a passion for building community. Originally from Fargo, North Dakota, she graduated from Kenyon College with a Bachelor of Arts in Film and Political Science. Music is one of her lifelong passions, and she plays clarinet with the Gay Freedom Band of Los Angeles and the Symphony of the Verdugos. Mia organizes with Nikkei Progressives, an activism organization based in Little Tokyo, and was a Co-Chair for Okaeri, a Nikkei LGBTQ+ community. Mia also enjoys reading, taking pottery classes, and going to karaoke.

Reiko Barnett - I am a Japanese American mom to my daughter who identifies as queer. I appreciate how she has invited me into her community, widening my world. Being with other parent allies at Okaeri has helped me understand and love her even more. Life is a journey; not linear or predictable, but worth every bumpy ride to unknown places.

Mitsuko 三津子 Brooks is a 1.5 generation mail artist & archivist of mixed settler Japanese and European descent living in Lenapehoking. She received her BFA from Cooper Union, MFA from UCLA, and MLIS from CUNY Queens College. Her work has been featured in exhibitions at Sikkema Jenkins, The Hammer Museum, and The Japanese American National Museum of San Jose, among others. She has participated in residencies at EFA, Wassaic Project and LMCC, and was awarded a grant from the Edward & Sally Van Lier Fellowship. Brooks' work is in the permanent collections of the Smithsonian's Archive of American Art.

Marilou Mariko Carrera (they/siyá/she) is a queer Filipinx-Okinawan cultural worker participating from the area called Chicago on Odawa, Ojibwe, and Potawatomi lands. An emerging artist with foundations in healthcare, organizing, and advocacy, they root largely in the creative practices of writing and movement as pathways and practices for personal and collective power, sharing stories, and healing. Their current preoccupations include Kali martial arts, slowness, queer storytelling, body sovereignty, textile arts, and reading. Their writings have been published in Sobbing in Seafood City (Sampaguita Press), Beyond the Margins (Oregon Humanities), and A Call to Nursing (anthology).

C.K. is a SoCal native and NYC transplant navigating her mid-20s. She loves dancing, udon, and putting on a great outfit. Japanese identity and queer identity have defined much of her life until now, and they continue to crop up relentlessly in her art. This is her first time sharing visual work with the public. In the years to come, she looks forward to growing as a visual artist and sharing even more. Thank you, Okaeri!

Tsukuru Fors (he/they) is an Asian/Immigrant/Non-binary trans individual; all these identities are very important to him. He is an anti-nuclear/healthcare justice/trans rights activist. In a nutshell, though, he just wants to live in a world where everyone is free to pursue their dreams, while feeling safe and loved.

Keila Sachi Gaballo (they/she) is a queer, disabled indigenous Shimanchu-Ainu mama, artist and trauma-informed somatic expressive arts practitioner based in San Diego (Kumeyaay Lands). They have a passion for mental health education, diverse representation, and embodied social justice. She weaves these elements throughout her storytelling as an illustrator, hand-letterer, writer, and teacher.

Gabrielle Kazuko Nomura Gainor is a dancer, activist, and storyteller. Working with an intergenerational group of dancers, Gabrielle explores topics such as Asian representation in Hollywood, the incarceration of Japanese Americans, Sadako Sasaki's wish for peace, Shinto mythology, and the impact of Asian mothers, grandmothers, and aunties. Gabrielle's work has been featured in The Seattle Times and on local NPR affiliate KUOW. The community-engagement work Gabrielle led for Seattle Opera's *Madame Butterfly* was praised as a "helpful model" in The New York Times. Gabrielle is the descendent of ancestors from Ireland, the Philippines, and Japan. Learn more at gabriellekazuko.com.

Alden M. Hayashi is a *Sansei* who was born and raised in Honolulu but now lives in Boston. After writing about science, technology, and business for more than thirty years, he has recently begun writing fiction and essays to preserve stories of the *Nikkei* experience. His first novel—*Two Nails, One Love*—was published by Black Rose Writing in 2021, and his short stories have appeared in the Baltimore Review, The Gordon Square Review, and the Bamboo Ridge journal.

Tomo Hirai is a *Shin-Nisei* Japanese American born and raised in the San Francisco Bay Area. She is a reporter for the Nichi Bei News in San Francisco and a freelance diversity consultant for tabletop games. She has seven girlfriends located throughout the world in the event she must flee either her immediate home, the state of California, the West Coast, the United States, or the continent due to being a trans woman.

Momo Hoshi (they/she) is a *Shin-Nisei* multi-instrumental musician, illustrator, and voice over artist. Though they don't typically consider themselves a writer, in their undergraduate career Momo wrote a thesis about *Shin-Nikkei* jazz musicians. During the day, Momo works in higher education to pursue their passion for supporting the mental and emotional wellbeing of young people. As a musician, Momo plays in symphonic orchestras, pit orchestras, chamber groups, and even in an R&B/soul/funk cover band! As an artist, Momo is always looking for new opportunities for growth and collaboration.

Carl Ichikawa is a *Sansei* living in Chicago and proud father of two adult daughters who are members of the LGBTQ+ community. Member of local Buddhist temple and ally to those seeking support, especially parents.

Wayne Itoga (He/Him/His). Divorced (from a guy). Single Dad. Old-fashioned cisgendered gay man. Bamboo ceilinged bureaucrat. Still coming out. Still finding my voice & learning how to use it. Still learning to navigate. Still liberating myself and making hay while I can still appreciate the sunshine, and pissing people off (unintentionally) all along the way. What can I say? It's a process.

Stacia Kato-Takayesu is the proud mama bear of a transgender daughter. Had it not been for SGV API PFLAG and all the families who tread this journey before, she isn't sure where she and her daughter would be now. She is happy to serve as a board member and visible community advocate.

Jessica Miyeko Kawamura's fondest memories are being a kid with her *Nisei* grandpa, hanging out in West Berkeley. She is deeply grateful for everyone who has helped raise her, from *Sansei* community leaders in the Bay Area and Asian American organizers in New York City, from queer friends in Atlanta to BIPOC church elders in LA and Hawai'i. Jessica currently resides outside Honolulu with her partner Kyle, their extended families, and their French bulldog Speedy. During her free time, she enjoys sewing classes, *bon* dances, beach days, and old episodes of *RuPaul's Drag Race*.

Hatsu Keith (he/him) is a queer bilingual Japanese American community leader. With 20 years of professional experience, he now works as an intercultural management consultant, supporting HR teams better recruit, engage, & retain their diverse workforce. Hatsu Keith served as a national Pride program director for the North American Association of Asian Professionals, invited to speak at Bain & Co., Movember Foundation, and Chambers of Commerce, and consulted for global brands like Toyota & Disney. Hatsu Keith wishes there was an organization like Okaeri growing up. He is honored to be included in the inaugural Okaeri book alongside kindred LGBTQ+ siblings, parents, & allies.

Rino Kodama is a nonbinary *Shin-Nisei* artist and organizer based in Los Angeles, originally from the Bay Area. I received my Bachelor of Arts in Fine Art at University of California in Los Angeles, and minored in Asian American studies. When I am not working as Okaeri's Tech & Media Marketing Coordinator and Okaeri Connects! Co-facilitator, you can find me in my backyard ceramic studio hand building sculptures and vases. I am passionate in helping shape a compassionate Japanese American community that is able to hold our queer and trans multiplicities and expansiveness.

Patty Kunitsugu is a *Sansei Nikkei* senior, in her early 70s. She worked as a technologist for 35 years, and in her 20s, was a trailblazing woman in the trades as a union carpenter. She was born and raised in Seattle, Washington. Living as a lesbian and being a part of the LGBTQ+ community in the 1960s was difficult due to homophobia and because the *Nikkei* community did not support LGBTQ+ members. This fueled Kunitsugu to be an activist, help others and advocate for human rights. She has lived with her Jewish wife for 46 years.

Ian Martyn (he/him) is a *Yonsei*, half-Japanese American whose family, from Ishikawa and Hiroshima prefectures, was incarcerated at Rohwer, Arkansas, where his mother was born. He graduated from Crossroads School in Santa Monica, subsequently earning a B.A. in Linguistics and Anthropology from UCLA and an M.A. in Ethnomusicology from UC Davis. He is a composer, arranger, and musician whose music can be found on streaming services. When he is not making music, he enjoys music from around the world, computer programming, gardening, nature photography, languages, and genealogy. He is also involved in JAMP and Okaeri Connects. https://linktr.ee/IanMartyn

Nikiko Masumoto (she/her) is an organic farmer, memory keeper, and artist. She is *Yonsei* and gets to touch the same soil her great-grandparents worked in California where Masumoto Family Farm grows organic nectarines, apricots, peaches and grapes for raisins. With her family, she's co-authored 2 books: Changing Season and The Perfect Peach, and has a children's book forthcoming. She activates her facilitation, leadership, and creative skills as a performer and leader in Yonsei Memory Project and as staff of the Center for Performance and Civic Practice. Her most cherished value is courage and most important practice is listening.

Michael Matsuno, DMA, is a flutist and educator based in Los Angeles, CA. He performs a variety of styles ranging from classical and experimental music, to improvisation and poetry. Michael's dissertation, in press, is a biography of the California E.A.R. Unit, one LA's first independent contemporary music ensembles. Drawing from interviews and archives, this writing shows some of the complex relationships between musicians and classical music institutions at the end of the 20th century. His other research explores topics in neurodiversity and daily life, and has been published in Psychology of Music and Naxos Musicology International. Michael holds teaching positions at CalArts,

Chapman University, and the Youth Orchestra of Los Angeles.

Kai Mita is currently pursuing a Master's in Management with a specialization in Business Data Management at the University of Illinois, Urbana-Champaign. My hobbies are traveling, photography, and attending concerts/festivals. I look forward to helping and learning more from the Japanese and LGBTQ+ communities.

kris mizutani (they/she), a *Yonsei* community organizer and proud Californian, is a product of the California public education system, and currently lives in northern California. They organize regularly with Omusubi, a fun and caring Bay Area-based group for queer women, non-binary and trans persons of Japanese descent. kris is a long-time volunteer with the Asian Pacific Islander Queer Women and Transgender Community (APIQWTC), and belongs to the Mugworts collective, a QTBIPOC-run healing and wealth redistribution project. kris is interested in the intersections of Buddhism and modern science. They love to get lost, wander, campfire-stargaze, and find connections in even the most mundane places.

Sam Nakahira is a comic artist and illustrator from Los Angeles. She makes art around overlooked histories, dreams, the natural world, and more. Her graphic novel, Ruth Asawa: An Artist Takes Shape, will be published in March 2024 by the Getty and Abrams Books.

Dane Nakama is a Japanese-Uchinanchu ceramicist, painter, and educator from Oʻahu, Hawaiʻi, currently based in the land of the Tongva nation in Los Angeles, California. Nakama addresses subjects of cultural hybridity, settler colonialism, and ancestral knowledge through the dreamy multicultural aesthetic of their childhood. They are also one of the founding members of fishschool Hawaiʻi education space and ceramics studio. Nakama received a BFA from the California Institute of the Arts and is a current UCLA MFA candidate in ceramics. They have taught workshops and participated in numerous group/solo exhibitions in Hawaiʻi, Los Angeles, Miami, & Tokyo.

Judy Yushin Nakatomi (she/we), mother, partner, kin, writer and community cultivator. She practices in her root, ancestral tradition, Jodo Shinshu and serves as a certified Minister's Assistant. Judy received ordination from the Plum Village Community of Engaged Buddhism of Thich Nhat Hanh. Learning and exploring from trauma sensitive teachers, Dr. Satsuki Ina, Resmaa Menakem, and Dr. Gabor Mate are current core ingredients to stay centered while becoming an advocate of inclusivity and justice. In an earlier chapter, Judy served as a special assistant to a member of congress. She is co-founder of a specialty Japanese tea company.

Jeri Okamoto-Tanaka, long-time supporter of Okaeri, is a *Sansei* serving as the Lay Leader of the West Los Angeles United Methodist Church, an LGBTQiA+ reconciling and affirming historic Japanese American congregation. With a Master of Divinity from the Claremont School of Theology and Juris Doctor from Loyola Law School, she centers her life and ministry on love, compassion, and social justice. She served her seminary field education at the 580 Café/Wesley Foundation Serving UCLA, an affirming QBIPOC, interfaith, and immigrant welcoming campus ministry. She is the mother of two daughters and auntie to beloved LGBTQiA+ family and friends.

Sakura Okubo is a *Nisei* transgender woman born and raised in Chicago, Illinois. Her parents immigrated from Hiroshima, Japan to Chicago. Sakura attended the University of Illinois at Chicago and graduated with a bachelor's degree and master's degree in Electrical Engineering. She also has a CompTIA certification in A+ and Network+ for computer repairs. In 2015, she was diagnosed with paranoid schizophrenia and PTSD. Sakura enjoys anime and manga. She used to play clarinet and piano and still enjoys all kinds of music today. This essay is the first time she has written her life story.

Scott Oshima is a Seattle-based artist and activist whose work unearths the personal and political history in our city streets and the futures they create. They have exhibited and performed at The Museum of Contemporary Art, Los Angeles; Japanese American Cultural & Community Center, Los Angeles; LA Contemporary Archive; and Human Resources LA. Three books of their photography, art, and writing have been published by No Style Press. They can often be found singing songs to the freeways, picking grapefruits from 150 year old trees in Little Tokyo, and laughing a lot and loudly.

eri oura (they/them) is a queer GNC *Sansei* born & raised in Honolulu, Hawai'i. eri is a passionate resource mobilizer and advocate for racial and gender justice. their community organizing experience is deeply rooted in supporting Hawaiian Sovereignty & de-militarization movements. eri is the Development Manager at Lavender Phoenix, an intergenerational TQAPI movement building & leadership development organization based in SF, where they lead efforts to mobilize resources for strategic systemic change. You can find them swimming in the rivers & lakes of the Sacramento area and ocean beaches. eri is the pawrent to the sweetest dog & cat duo, Elton Butterfly & Demi Butterfly!

Pepu - I always loved to draw and wanted to become a *manga* artist up until I was 18. I realized I didn't have what it took to become a *mangaka* and studied English instead. Over a number of decades, I worked for different companies in Tokyo, always utilizing English. I moved to Los Angeles in 2001 with my husband. Now I work with Japanese companies, finding great joy in helping their employees and families navigate life in the U.S. My husband and I are truly fortunate to have a wonderful son and two of the cutest cats in the world.

anaïs peterson (no pronouns) is a *Yonsei* organizer and artist based in pittsburgh, pa. anaïs writes in black pen and garamond size 11 and posts from @anais_pgh. anaïs' chapbook, "for the joy of it" is available on sundress publication's website—you can find a full list of anaïs' publications and more information at: anaispeterson.weebly.com.

Justen Quan is a fourth generation Japanese American (*Yonsei*) who grew up in Sacramento, California. Justen grew up attending the Buddhist Church of Sacramento and played basketball in the Japanese American leagues. He later attended UCLA and graduated with a degree in Civil & Environmental Engineering. He now resides in Irvine, California with his partner, Jon, and their dog, Kiko. Justen enjoys spending time with family and friends, boba, r&b music, going to the gym/being active, cooking, finding good places to eat, and learning Spanish.

Mariko Rooks - A longtime member of the Southern California Japanese American community, Mariko serves on the Little Tokyo Towers & Little Tokyo Towers Foundation Boards and was named one of Japanese American National Museum's "30 Under 30 Community Changemakers" in 2021. Mariko also had the privilege of serving as a committee member for Okaeri's first Queer Obon in 2023. In her spare time, she plays taiko with Kinnara and dances with Nippon Minyo Kenkyukai, Hoshun Kai. Previous writing: JookSongs, Discover Nikkei, Porchwater Press, Changing Wxman Collective.

Stacey Sagara Shigaya (she/her) - I am a 3rd generation JA, born and raised in Denver, CO and am the Executive Director for Sakura Foundation, a nonprofit whose mission is to celebrate and share Japanese and Japanese American culture and heritage in order to promote a more compassionate, resilient, & equitable society. My greatest source of joy and pride is being the proud mom of my two adult kids, one of whom is a member of the LGBTQ+ community.

Ken Takeuchi is a Japanese filmmaker, composer, and Emmy winning re-recording mixer with a focus on social justice. In 1987, Ken arrived in Muskegon, MI., as an exchange student. He thrived in school band as a talented drummer, winning numerous competitions. At Berklee College of Music, Ken excelled as a film scoring major, winning the third place in the final dissertation project. Moving to NYC in 1994, he joined a premiere sound studio, Onomatopoeia, Inc. as lead engineer. His first short documentary, "GAPIMNY15" was an official selection at Aomori Int'l LGBT Film Festival in 2007.

Ellen Tanouye is a former PC(USA) pastor who came out of the closet 12 years ago. She graduated from SFTS in 1995, served in two Asian churches, one in the Bay Area and one in the Central Valley. She is currently a board member and volunteer clergy at Reflection MCC church in Folsom CA. She loves to sing and play the piano; she has lead retreats and planned conferences; she has written Parenting curriculum, Church school curriculum for youth on Sexuality and Gender and devotionals for many years; she loves to preach and teach and lead in worship.

Jill Togawa (she/they), *Yonsei* from and rooted in Hawai'i, is a choreographer, dancer, storyteller, community change maker, lover of family and friends, and AT (alexander technique) teacher. They have always loved writing though they have not called themself a writer since elementary school. After founding Purple Moon in 1992, to create work that illuminated experiences of lesbians and women of color, she became inspired to use words alongside dances in multi-disciplinary collaboration. Jill is passionate about making visible the less visible and telling unheard stories, using the arts and performance as a vehicle for healing and peace in our society.

Daniel Tomita (he/him) is a *Shin-Nisei* who was born and raised in Southern California. He received his Bachelor of Fine Arts in Graphic Design from California State University, Long Beach and has been a professional graphic designer for over 15 years. He currently works for Walt Disney Imagineering creating graphics and signage for Disneyland, where he most recently utilized his (admittedly limited) bilingual skills to help bring the fictional world of San Fransokyo to life. He would also like to express his sincere gratitude for the generosity of spirit and acceptance shown to him by all of his Okaeri colleagues and family—love you all. Learn more at danieltomita.com

Joseph Tsuboi (he/they) is a queer, mixed race, multi-generational *Nikkei* person based on Tongva land. As a recent graduate in Asian American Studies, Joseph researched Asian American organizing spaces in the greater Los Angeles area and their techniques towards cross-community solidarity. Grounded in oral history and archival document analysis, Joseph has made sense of the uncertainties of the COVID-19 pandemic through investing in storytelling as a means of community care. Joseph works in Asian American non-profit spaces as a program coordinator and serves on Vigilant Love's steering committee. Joseph's creative practices include body movement and yoga, fashion and skincare, and cooking dishes reminiscent of his grandmother.

Deena Umeda is a UCSB graduate with a degree in Asian American Studies. During her time in college, she worked on the Nikkei Student Union board as the Vice-President and Culture Night Director. She wrote and directed the UCSB Nikkei Culture Night play *Unearthed*. She is passionate about creating space for the Japanese American and LGBTQ+ communities as well as sharing their histories. During her free time she enjoys doing her makeup, throwing dinner parties with her friends, and picking up different hobbies such as: felting, gardening, biking, and anything else she sets her mind to.

Cody Uyeda is a fourth generation Japanese American from Southern California. He received his BA and JD from the University of Southern California, and also holds a Masters in Education from the Harvard Graduate School of Education. He is currently Okaeri's Program & Admin Coordinator, and previously came from a background in the education, research, and legal fields. He is passionate about supporting the Japanese American community, as well as exploring culture, arts, and the outdoors.

Anne Watanabe (she/her) is a queer femme *Yonsei* and *Shin-Nisei* nurse, organizer, peer counselor, and writer. She organizes with Nikkei Uprising, a *Nikkei* collective that organizes for collective liberation with an abolitionist and anti-imperialist lens, but originally found *Nikkei* community through queerness. She loves when poetry helps us to choose feeling over numbness, to shrink/stretch time, and witness each other and ourselves.

Bill Watanabe was the founding Executive Director of the Little Tokyo Service Center, a multi-purpose community service agency in downtown LA's Little Tokyo historic neighborhood. He is also the convener of the APIA's for Christian Social Justice and a member of Evergreen Baptist Church of the San Gabriel Valley. The opinions and viewpoints shared in his piece are strictly his own.

Kazumi Yamaguchi grew up in Honolulu, Hawai'i and currently serves as the Director of Transgender Health and Support Services for St. John's Community Health in Los Angeles. Kazumi's mission is to provide and improve access to culturally competent and affirming healthcare for the Transgender, Gender Non-Conforming, and Non-Binary communities locally and nationwide, with an emphasis on HIV prevention and education, Substance use and Recovery, and Mental Health. Kazumi envisions a future where transgender individuals can live freely and authentically, without fear of prejudice or discrimination.

Ion Yamazaki currently lives and works in Wichita, Kansas. Their work explores Japan's imperialism and patriarchy with video, performance, installation, and sculpture to construct possibilities to existing narratives. Intertwining history, trauma, reality, and dream, they actualize imagined spaces through which they understand their identity and place on Earth.

はな - 豊かな空想の世界を持つトランスジェンダーの娘と、その娘を深く愛する夫と、雪の降る町に住んでいます。

RESOURCES

As a small nonprofit, our knowledge and expertise only extend so far. Therefore, we'd like to share additional resources, articles, and organizations focused on the *Nikkei* and API LGBTQ+ communities for those looking to learn more or get involved in the community.

Please visit **https://www.okaeri.org** to view our resources page. This resource list is intended to be a starting point and is not comprehensive of all available resources.

SUPPORT OKAERI

As a nonprofit organization, Okaeri relies on the generosity of donors, patrons, and community members. Donations to Okaeri are tax-deductible as a gift under Okaeri's fiscal sponsor LTSC's (Little Tokyo Service Center) nonprofit 501(c)3 status. To make a donation to Okaeri, please visit the donations page on the Okaeri website or contact us directly.

For all inquiries regarding this publication or Okaeri in general, please contact us through our website **okaeri.org** or at: **info@okaeri.org**.

Okaeri
- A NIKKEI LGBTQ+ COMMUNITY -

www.ingramcontent.com/pod-product-compliance
Lightning Source LLC
Chambersburg PA
CBHW041738300726
48978CB00006B/148